To Ed,

Thank you for
All you have done
for this magnificent
Profession!

All good wishes
for your
continued
Success

PROFITABLE
PRACTICE

WHY A DENTAL PRACTICE
IS AN EXCEPTIONAL INVESTMENT

Timothy A. Brown

Sarah K. Lynch

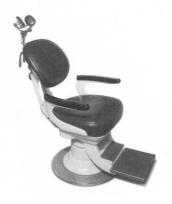

ECW Press

Published by ECW Press, 2120 Queen Street East, Suite 200,
Toronto, Ontario, Canada M4E 1E2
416.694.3348 / info@ecwpress.com

LIBRARY AND ARCHIVES CANADA CATALOGUING IN PUBLICATION

Brown, Timothy A
Profitable practice : why a dental practice is an exceptional
investment / Timothy A. Brown, Sarah Lynch.

Includes bibliographical references.
ISBN 978-1-77041-026-8

1. Dental offices—Canada—Management.
2. Dentistry—Practice—Canada.
I. Lynch, Sarah, 1960- II. Title.

RK58.7.C3B76 2011   651'.961760971   C2010-906815-7

Cover and text design: Tania Craan
Cover image © Koksharov Dmitry
Typesetting: Mary Bowness
Printing: Thomson-Shore   1   2   3   4   5

PRINTED AND BOUND IN THE UNITED STATES

ECW PRESS
ecwpress.com

This book is dedicated to the work of our fathers, Roy Brown and Jim Kasper. Their vision, determination, and hard work has allowed successful dental practices to be transferred in an orderly fashion to aspiring practitioners dedicated to the delivery of first-rate dental care.

"The physician should know what the physician before him has known, if he does not want to defraud himself and others."
— HIPPOCRATES

Table of Contents

"You don't write because you want to say something; you write because you've got something to say."
— F. SCOTT FITZGERALD

Our careers have been a product of our fathers' life work. This book is meant to honor them and our mothers, Joan and Rosemary, who supported them and helped build their companies. With *Profitable Practice* we also hope to continue their goal of allowing dentists "to retire with dignity."

We wish to thank the following dentists for their inspiration over the last twenty years: Dr. Howard Rocket, Dr. Jerry Isenberg, Dr. John Wilson, Dr. John Badger, Dr. Jeff Williams, Dr. Wayne Raborn, Dr. Marcia Boyd, Dr. Bob Watson, Dr. Tony Bates, Dr. Craig Leffingwell, Dr. Joseph Wasileski, Dr. Jerry Scholl, Dr. Gary Morris, Drs. Ken and Kathleen Hale, Dr. Dwight Stowell and especially our dear friend Dr. Roger Ellis.

As well, with thanks to Dr. Bruce Glazer, who graciously gave me a copy of the greatest text I have ever read about dental practice management, written by George Wood Clapp, D.D.S., in 1916 and entitled *Profitable Practice.*

We are indebted to G. Christen and Peter M. Pronych for documenting the great history of Painless Parker. Many references to Parker's fascinating history are contained in this book.

Timothy Brown: I am deeply grateful for the aid and ideas provided by Harry van Bommel, my friend Barbara Martin, my sisters, Lanee Brown and Sally Brown, my patient wife, Sandy Evans, my very good friend and editor, Jim Ruddy and my neighbor (the "millionaire" next door) Andre Frehn. Sarah Lynch: I would like to thank my partner and brother, Dave Kasper, colleague Jason Anderson, and my supportive husband Nate Lynch. Thanks to the people at ECW Press, especially Jennifer Knoch, for their advice and guidance. Without all of their help this book would not have been completed.

The majority of the text is a collection of wise anecdotes and experiences given by dentists in the course of the research of this book. In essence, it constitutes dentists giving advice to other dentists. The advice was offered freely and candidly in order to alert other dentists to some of the pitfalls of a dental practice. In short, these dentists wanted others to benefit from their experiences and mistakes.

Also, this book is intended to be a guideline to recent dental graduates. ROI Corporation and Jim Kasper Associates, LLC wish you aspiring dentists great success. In addition, veteran dentists well into the middle stages of their career will find many good suggestions and best practices that may be of assistance, or at least confirm what they already know. Lastly, dentists in the final stages of their career will find sound advice on how to sell their practice and retire with dignity.

One cannot predict the future while ignoring the past. *Profitable Practice: Why a Dental Practice Is an Exceptional Investment* offers the dental practitioners and others interested in this remarkable profession some insight into what is possible to achieve within the scope of a lifetime of professional practice.

Why does one dental practitioner gross three times as much as his equally qualified colleague on the same side of the street? Where are the best opportunities to practice today? What is the future of practice in the U.S. in the twenty-first century? How does increasing government involvement in healthcare impact the dental practice today and in the future?

These are a few of the questions which hopefully can be answered by this well documented review of one of the most challenging and rewarding medical specialties.

Enjoy and prosper!

JIM KASPER

"Those Were the Days"

In the 1950s, when I met with dentists who had just graduated, their primary concern was what location to select to start a new practice. The major consideration was: do you want to set up an office near to where you want to live or to set up where you are needed? Since new patient flow was more than adequate almost everywhere, most dentists chose to go to where they wanted to live. The established dentists of Canada were booked solid for many months in advance. Most enjoyed a relaxed workweek of nine to five, taking either Wednesday or Friday off, and rarely did a dentist work an evening or a weekend.

Fifty years ago more than 90% of dental school graduates were male. Since there were few plazas, shopping centres or medical dental offices, they looked for offices on the second floor above an existing store.

The ideal set-up was a corner office with windows on both corners and room on the exterior wall for advertising their practice. Some landlords were hesitant to lease or rent to a dentist, as they were concerned about the potential plumbing problems that might occur and the damage that would result to the tenants below. However, dentists became prized tenants for two reasons: they were prompt with their rent payments, and they usually stayed twenty or more years in the same location. Still, the leaseholds were expensive as they needed small partitioned rooms with specialized plumbing and wiring. These specialized rooms proved challenging and costly. Landlords provided many of the required improvements and charged two to five dollars per square foot for prime locations.

The cost of opening a new office ranged from $7,000 to $10,000. A single operatory with new equipment cost about $5,000. This included a chair, delivery unit, x-ray, lights, cabinet, sterilization, compressor, lathe and darkroom tank. There weren't any Cavitrons, high-speed handpieces, pan x-rays or computers to be purchased. When the dentist's office was finished, he or she was usually fully booked within the first week of operation.

Staffing was without chair-side assistants or hygienists. The doctor required one receptionist/nurse who booked patients, collected fees, cleaned up and, if time allowed, would mix materials. The patient sat upright with an articulating head and footrest (like a barber's chair). The dentist stood up. The delivery unit was also an upright, floor-mounted device with an engine, a chair, two syringes (water and air), a cuspidor and a saliva injector. That's all.

Steel burrs were sold by the half gross; there were no carbide burrs. Slow speed engines with belts and handpieces ran at a maximum speed of 2000–5000 rpm. Dentists applied pressure as there were no lubricants or cooling when cutting was needed. Replacement of fillings was common because materials for anterior silicates and amalgam silicates or porcelains often washed out.

Fees were low. A filling cost from $5 to $9; an extraction was $5 to $10; dentures started at about $85; x-rays cost about $3 each. There was little or no endodontics, cosmetic surgery or implants.

A good day's gross was $400 to $500 resulting in an income of $80,000 to $100,000 per year with overhead of 40%. The size of most offices ranged between 500 and 750 square feet, with two operatories (one that was empty and unused for varying lengths of time), a small lab, a darkroom, both a business office and private office and a waiting room. Many dentists resisted equipping the second operatory because they could only treat one patient at a time. Eventually, it became efficient and profitable to have a nurse who could clean up one operatory and set up a patient in the other.

Practices were rarely bought or sold. Most practices simply closed due to retirement or health concerns. The location might merit the sale price of $5,000 for the used equipment and the traditional payment for goodwill was $1, only to make it legal!

In the late 1950s many changes slowly occurred and

then accelerated dramatically through the 1960s and 1970s. These changes included chair-side assistants and technical advances such as high-speed air turbines and wash field cooling spray. Time and motion and quadrant dentistry came into practice. Denturists and hygienists did much of the cleaning and mundane duties of the practice, leaving dentists to concentrate on the technical and complicated aspects. At the same time, dental insurance plans paid for more treatments than before.

Today, 60 years later, the result of those changes and many others is staggering. A brand new dental office is usually 1,500 to 2,000 square feet, with four to six operatories, and built with superior equipment for associates and hygienists. Annual gross now ranges from $750,000 to over $1 million. The key to a successful new practice is constant new patient flow — and the competition for new patients is fierce!

Most dentists are being advised by their bankers and accountants to buy an established practice if only to benefit from immediate cash flow. This ensures steady, daily patient flow from the first day and avoids many of the pitfalls of high set-up costs and rents. The typical established practice now sells for $750,000 to over $1 million dollars.

Ah, to think back to the 1950s — those were the days . . .

ROY BROWN

Roy Brown is the Chairman Emeritus of ROI Corporation, Canada's largest dental practice appraiser and broker.

Dentistry as a Business

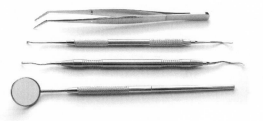

CHAPTER 1

The History of Dental Practice Management

When Did the First Practice Manager Offer Advice to a Dentist?

There are no industry records that show practice management was ever seen as a necessary course of study in any schools of dentistry, nor was it valued as a criterion of a successful practice. The first advice given to a dentist was likely from a spouse or a banker, hardly experts in dental practice management. Once in practice, dentists would typically look to their colleagues for tips on how to build a practice. This process did not guarantee success.

Who Then Pioneered the Modern Practice Management Industry?

Dr. Clapp's book entitled *Profitable Practice*, written in 1916, offered the following advice:

"Dentistry as means of service is a profession; as a means of livelihood it is a business."

Further, in his opening remarks, Clapp thanked those who gave him guidance:

"May their efforts speed the day when the discussion of the business elements in practice will receive the same full, free and beneficial discussion that is now accorded to technical questions. Then will dawn the day of fees that are fair to patients and to dentists."

Clearly, these are wise words that foresee the need for professional advice.

Definition of Practice Management

While there is no one industry definition that is acceptable to all, the following provides a working statement for the purposes of this book:

"The art and science of running a profitable dental practice."

Painless Parker (a.k.a. Edgar Randolph), a man famous for pioneering the advertising of dental services to America in the early 1900s, has his definition:

"You have to be organized, systematized, capitalized, advertised, standardized, and specialized. These are the major principles of business economics."

Painless Parker idolized P.T. Barnum, the owner of the world's greatest circus. Barnum offered this advice to Painless:

"The great secret of anything is to get a hearing. Half the object is gained when the audience is assembled."

Arthur Schopenhauer, the famous German philosopher of the nineteenth century, wrote:

"If you want to achieve something in business, in writing, in painting, you must follow the rules without knowing them."

These words ring true today. Practice management is not any different now than it was in the early years of dentistry.

The four simple steps to successful practice management are:

1. Greet the patient.
2. Treat the patient.
3. Bill and collect fees.
4. Remind them to return and repeat the process.

Advertising is an essential promotional tool to expand a dental practice. Treating the patient effectively is the sole responsibility of the dentist. Billing and collecting, and then reminding them to return for continuing treatments (recall programs), are the responsibilities of all the staff in the modern dental practice.

Who Then Is the Practice Manager?

Some dentists do employ office managers to perform the majority of day-to-day routine requirements, but ultimately it is the dentist, as owner of the practice, who is the official practice manager. He/she must decide on the key elements of how to position the practice in the marketplace, given the many variables that Painless Parker mentions:

1. *Organization* — This involves the selection of financial record-keeping systems, charting systems and recall systems.

2. *Systemization* — This mandates integrating the above organizational tools into a highly repetitive and accurate process.

3. *Capitalization* — This requires securing financial resources from personal, family or financial institutions to adequately equip the practice with the tools of the trade necessary to deliver service in a timely and profitable fashion.

4. *Advertising* — This requires promoting your service to the public and attracting people to your unique offering as opposed to other dental practices.

5. *Standardization* — This necessitates perfecting the delivery systems in all regards so that the final results are consistent with the intended service level offering.

6. *Specialization* — This involves mastering the dental service and offering that service at the highest level possible. It also involves recognizing when a dental practice cannot meet the needs of the patient and recommending a dental practice that can.

CHAPTER 2

The History of Jim Kasper Associates and the Birth of Dental Practice Brokerage in the U.S.

Jim Kasper began his career working with dentists in 1955. Starting out in the U.S. Coast Guard as a dental technician, he went on to selling dental equipment and instruments in 1960 to dentists in New England and New York State, setting up many dentists with their first private practice. Jim Kasper sold his first practice in 1963 for the tidy sum of $3,500 in South Deerfield, Massachusetts. His client, a dentist with a terminal medical condition, said to Jim, "You helped me get started now, now I need you to help get me out." There were no practice appraisers or brokers around in those days so it was pretty much the value of some equipment and that was it. Jim went on to selling his equipment and instrument business in the 1970s and went into practice management with a company called Sycom. Sycom sold the first in office computer systems, practice management consulting and a service still remembered as PBP (Professional Budget Plan).

When Sycom decided to pull out of the practice management consulting and computer business in 1981, Jim started NCCD Consulting, and Jim Kasper Associates, LLC thus evolved. He was a well known practice management consultant in the Northeast and helped many dentists achieve their goals and dreams. He repeatedly encountered several of his dental clients wanting to retire or grow their practice with associates. Jim embraced the opportunity and started offering appraisal services and brokerage to his clients. Through networking at dental meetings around the country, Jim got involved with Practice Valuation Study Group as it began in 1985 when a handful of brokers, accountants and dentists from around the country started getting together to share methodologies and nuances involved in appraising dental practices and selling them. From there, the industry of dental practice brokerage and appraisal evolved into a fine art. In the early years, banks would only finance equipment purchases and the seller of the practice would also have to hold a secondary note for any "goodwill" in the sale of the dental practice. Jim and his colleagues spent several years and countless hours speaking with bankers to convince them to finance the whole transaction and base their lending decisions on cash flow of the practice, good credit, character and the value of a dental degree.

Persistance paid off and finally the industry started

to see 100% financing on practices in 1995. As a result there are now several well established direct cash flow lenders servicing the U.S. and Canada supporting the ongoing needs of our dental clients. It is now 2011, and Jim Kasper's legacy continues thirty years later!

CHAPTER 3

The History of ROI Corporation

The author's father, Roy Brown, began selling dental supplies in 1948, at the age of 18. He joined the Associated Dentists Cooperative (ADC) as a junior salesman and was assigned a territory based out of London, Ontario. The ADC was owned and managed by a revolving board of directors that consisted almost exclusively of dentists.

The ADC was founded in response to an investigation by the Canadian Department of Justice to determine if an alleged combine in the manufacture and sale of dental supplies existed within Canada. The July 28, 1947, report, submitted by the Right Honourable J.L. Ilsley, K.C., Minister of Justice, concluded the following:

> *"A combine exists in the distribution and sale of dental supplies in Canada."*

The ADC was formed because a group of entrepreneurial dentists decided to take the purchase and distribution of dental supplies into their own hands. The ADC was a for-profit cooperative that redistributed dividends to the shareholders — most of whom were dentists who purchased their goods from the company.

During Roy Brown's 26-year career with the ADC, he pioneered many services of the profession. The ADC owned the first equipment-leasing company. He was successful in bringing Siemens dental equipment (now Sirona) to Canada. Many dentists will recognize the famous 50 KV x-ray units that are still in use today, almost 40 years later!

As Roy worked his way up to general manager and then president, he became aware that many of the board member dentists were aging and retirement was nearing.

Who would take over their established practices?

After a lengthy career with the ADC, later named Healthco in the early 1970s, Roy Brown wanted to assist dentists to leave their practices with dignity and a profit — thus he formed ROI Management (later renamed ROI Corporation) in 1974.

At first dentists were skeptical. Until then, when dentists retired they simply closed the doors, stored the equipment, terminated staff and advised patients to seek treatment elsewhere. There were very few "transitions" from one dentist to another, and rarely was a practice actually sold.

In 1974, Roy met with one of the most established and successful dentists in Toronto. This dentist was frustrated at the prospect of shutting down his very well-equipped and successful practice. He commissioned Roy to act as his agent and to find him a replacement dentist to take over. He set his asking price at $28,000.

Later that year, Roy identified a suitable dentist, a contract was negotiated, and what appears to be the very first "brokered" sale of a dental practice was documented in Canada. The price paid? Exactly $28,000!

CHAPTER 4

The Dentist
as Business Person

* *

"I'm not a good business person."

Sadly, this is a common statement made by dentists. This belief is largely untrue and only perpetuates the myth of business incompetence with regard to dentists.

There are many clever and well-trained individuals who sell to the dental profession. Most are reputable persons who are partnered with the profession for mutual success. Others are less than reputable and find that dentists are often easy prey for their gimmicks and wares.

> *"Truth carried to an extreme may become an untruth, and some of the speakers and writers who have grown up with the pale of the code have taken some principles to nonsensical extremes which have been very harmful to dentists who have been misled thereby."*
> — GEORGE WOOD CLAPP

"Making the simple complicated is commonplace: making the complicated simple, awesomely simple — that's creativity."

— CHARLES MINGUS

Why Do Some Dentists Believe They Are Not Good Business People?

The notion starts in university and then is perpetuated by the dentists themselves and their advisors. Dentists often enter dental school with ideals and dreams of what dentistry will be like. They have visions of running a small business, having loyal staff and patients who adore them, working with their hands and earning an above average income.

The economics of a dental practice are largely ignored and the science of dentistry becomes the entire focus of the curriculum. The business of dentistry is rarely discussed at this formative stage and service to patients dominates the teaching of dental students.

This is, perhaps, as it should be.

When Should Dental Economics Be Taught to Dental Students?

Research interviews with hundreds of dentists reveal that they never received instruction in sound business practices. Virtually all the dentists who graduated from the 1950s to the early 2000s state that they were inadequately prepared and lacked confidence in their ability to run a dental practice.

The purchase of an established practice has become fashionable, partly due to the fact that the business has been up and running for many years. Thus the formation of the business model is much less of a challenge to the dentist who buys a practice.

> *"The young dentist without commercial experience who can get a position in an office where good business and professional methods are practiced is usually much better off, in the end, than he who starts out 'on his own.'"*
> — GEORGE WOOD CLAPP

While Clapp had many opinions on how to establish a dental practice, his advice to find a position in an existing office was, and still is, the best advice that a young graduate can follow.

Why try to learn all the secrets of successful practice when hundreds of thousands have done it before you?

Dental schools train dentists to be competent. Working within a practice as an associate dentist will expose young dentists to the simplicity of the business model, after which they are prepared to confidently take over their own practice.

Advisors to the profession come in many forms and have varying degrees of knowledge and competency. However, the art and science of running a successful practice is best learned while on the job and from those who actually own a practice. Dental advisors profit from a dentist's need for their counsel, and some may even suggest that young dentists hand over this critical aspect of their business to them as they offer to take care of the business while the dentists focus on the dentistry.

In the end this becomes a foolhardy practice as ultimately dentists alone are responsible for their practices.

Certainly advisors should provide counsel on legal and financial matters such as the unknown aspects of taxation, but they should not become the official practice manager.

Many dentists who completely hand over the role of practice manager to third parties invariably regret having done so. One such dentist, who graduated in 1946, exemplifies what many other dentists have said:

> *"The patients are the practice, all the rest is just paperwork!"*
> — I. LIGHTMAN, D.D.S.

Who Is Qualified to Offer Practice Management Advice?

Most advisors, including the authors, have never worked a single day in a dental office — therefore, how can such advisors possibly understand what it's really like?

While this is true, reputable advisors have spent countless hours in many dental offices observing both good and bad practices. These advisors gather data and insight from across Canada and the U.S. The best advisors are aware of new developments and technical advances. These people are in the business of assessing successful dental and business practices in order to adequately evaluate what such practices are financially worth.

New dentists often underestimate their ability to start a new practice in a new area or location. They often put their trust in others to help them, sometimes with disastrous results.

Dentists are trained to measure precisely their clinical work. They work in small rooms, with small instruments, in a very small space (the mouth) and apply their skills in very small hand movements.

Practice management, on the other hand, requires broad vision and macroeconomic thinking. When the details of practice management are addressed and issues that require a wider perspective arise, dentists can become fixated on the minutiae and often overanalyze or dissect practice management issues to the extreme.

Running an exceptional practice is more than science; it is very much an art. It requires great people skills for dealing with staff and patients. Patients must perceive that the office is well run by qualified and caring individuals. They must have a sense of trust and confidence. Staff members must be made to feel a part of a team that respects each other and has a common goal of providing first-rate dental care. Staff members have to be encouraged and coached regularly to genuinely take pride in what they are doing and in communicating their concern for their patients. The working environment must be pleasing and amicable for all this to happen.

Dentists are much better trained to be scientists than artists. This is why they have such a large need for practice management training in dental school, and because it is lacking, this is also why dentists seek the help of "experts" to assist them. Perhaps this book can help to reduce the need for costly and often controversial practice managers.

CHAPTER 5

The Dental Consumer

. . . .

Will There Be Adequate Demand for the Dental Services in the Future?

In the 1960s some predicted dire consequences for dentists with the introduction of fluoride in the water treatment system. Some dentists even predicted their own demise.

Today, two generations later, dentistry is thriving! In 2010 the annual spending on dental care in the U.S. was $107.9 billion.* In part, this is due to improved technology allowing new and better procedures. As well, public education has instilled a need for greater dental care. Lastly, there has been a much greater demand in the highly lucrative area of cosmetic dentistry.

The primary dental consumer (the patient) is the baby boomer. Typically, this person is about fifty years

*SOURCE: cms.gov

of age and will have a huge impact on the dental practices for at least another twenty years! These men and women are entering their prime personal care spending years.

Research suggests that the total annual spending on dental care in the U.S. will reach $180.4 billion by the year 2019.* This will be largely a result of the baby boomers' desire to look better and their willingness to spend on themselves.

Unlike previous generations, boomers see dental cosmetics as an entitlement and an investment in themselves. Many patients are seeking instant gratification in this regard. This raises many ethical issues for some dentists.

Should they do procedures that would remove or alter perfectly good teeth simply for the sake of good looks? Should they deprive themselves of the lucrative fees they could charge for such treatments? Should they deny their patients' demands for dental cosmetics? Research indicates that it is unlikely that the demand for cosmetic procedures will diminish any time soon.

Where Are Dental Services in the Greatest Demand?

The leading indicator of demand for dental services is the ratio of dentists to the total population. Today, according to the ADA, the ratio of dentists to population is 1:1,804 and the ADA does not have an ideal number of people per dentist. The state of Maine, for example, has 2,178 people per dentist.**

Unfortunately, most methods of calculating ratios

*SOURCE: cms.gov annual estimates
**SOURCE: Survey on Dental Practice, ADA, 2008

are unreliable. They purely "count" the number of dentists registered to practice in a given parameter — usually a city or town. This number is then divided by the published population figures. This ignores several key factors:

- The actual equivalent full-time ratio of dentists (how many work a full-time schedule in that given area)
- The propensity of those dentists to continue in full-time practice for an unknown duration.

A few years back, a charming young dentist indicated that she would not move to a particular community because she had determined that there were too many dentists in the town already. When asked what her method was for determining this, she carefully explained that she had examined the telephone directory and the dental college listing of dentists. She then divided the number of names into the town's population figure (as provided by the town on their welcome sign while entering the community). She concluded that there was one dentist for every 1,500 people. This ratio was lower than the 1:2,000 ratio her professors had suggested was necessary to start a practice.

By chance, one of the authors happened to know all the dentists in that town, their ages and their work schedules. With this data, a calculation of the actual equivalent full-time dentists was made. A visit to the local government website revealed the current population was actually higher. The population sign had not been updated in years. With the corrected numbers, the actual ratio was 1:2,200 — almost 40% better than the young dentist had concluded.

Thus, when seeking a dental practice opportunity in any area, using names and population figures may not yield an accurate ratio. Our research suggests a deduction of 10% to 20% should be made from the names in the various directories for part-time and semi- or fully-retired dentists. Their names still appear even though they have retired or greatly reduced their workload.

Until the 1970s there was a limited but adequate supply of equivalent full-time (EFT) dentists in most regions. Then, for two decades, the dental schools increased class sizes, increasing the supply of dentists faster than the growth in population. Thus the number of dentists increased, mostly in the major cities.

A profile of the current graduates reveals that 85% of females (and the majority of all dental students are now female) show a strong preference for living in large cities and suburban areas, and if gender is removed, we see large majorities of new dentists are from cultures that prefer to stay in the larger cities for family and community reasons. This shift in the demographics of the graduating classes for the next decade will continue to have a serious impact upon ratios in the major cities.

For the foreseeable future, dentists will continue to choose to live and work in urban and suburban areas, thus limiting the EFT supply in rural and remote regions. This trend will continue to impact the sale prices of practices everywhere. Major city practices will remain valuable, while those practices situated in remote rural areas will likely decline in value.

In conclusion, overall demand for dental services will increase due to the needs of an aging population and the trend toward cosmetic dentistry. Consequently, dental practices are, and will remain, a very good investment in the major North American cities and suburbs for the foreseeable future.

CAREER MODELS

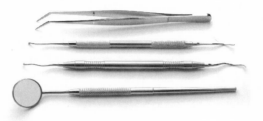

CHAPTER 6

The New Graduate Dentist and the Associate Experience

● ●

The long process of becoming a qualified dentist is over. Now what? Some dentists will go directly into postgraduate studies or residency programs. Others take a long-deserved vacation, but most will go into practice as an associate.

Associating has many advantages:

- *No additional financial burden* — The practice owner pays all the bills and invests in the facility and equipment; thus the new graduate has the opportunity to pay off student debts or to save for future needs.
- *Little management responsibility* — The practice owner is the practice manager; thus the associate is able to focus on building clinical competency and patient management skills.
- *Freedom to move on short notice and to pursue*

other opportunities — Most practice owners ask for one or two months' notice; unfortunately, many associates leave on very short notice. This practice is not recommended as it invariably creates hard feelings and potential future repercussions.

The disadvantages are:

• *Lack of authority for major decision making* — The practice owner controls the new graduate's schedule and patient flow — sometimes to the point where he/she is working at a much slower pace than desired.
• *A slowly increasing income curve* — It takes a year or two to earn the trust of the practice owner, staff and patients before the associate is working at the pace required to earn what is necessary for rapid debt reduction or savings.
• *Short notice terminations are common* when the associate and the practice owner have a different philosophy that leaves the associate out of work when he/she could be earning income.
• *Many associates work in multiple practices* as many practice owners can only offer two or three days of patient flow.

The alternatives are to set up a new office from scratch or to buy an established practice to eliminate these disadvantages. Historically, the new graduate is not ready for either of these commitments for at least three to five years. Thus, the associateship is the choice of the large majority, even with the obvious shortcomings.

There are only a handful of new graduates each year who feel confident and clinically adept enough to actually purchase a practice right out of dental school.

The Associate Buy-In (a.k.a. "Hire the Buyer")

Some associate positions are undertaken with the intent to buy into the practice at a later date. Some associate agreements have the time and price more or less agreed upon at the outset. Unfortunately, these intentions are often postponed or abandoned as the relationship between practice owner and associate develops. Like many marriages, the intentions are for a long-term commitment, but often this is not the case. People and professionals may grow apart in their plans and dreams and many agreements are broken off prematurely.

Practice owners are advised to avoid any promise of ownership when hiring an associate dentist. Practice owners often use the promise of ownership to attract a suitable associate. Usually, they expect the associate to work evenings, Fridays and weekends. They give the associate difficult patients and difficult procedures. A case in point involved a dentist who hired an associate for the above reasons. The associate demanded an ownership offering after one year. Reluctantly, the dentist conceded. However, after a short time, the arrangement made was unsatisfactory. The associate sued for a constructive dismissal and received a sizeable settlement.

Interviews with many young associates reveal they agree to a commitment to buy in because they want the position to gain experience and earn income. One unscrupulous associate admitted he had copied the computer records of the practice owner and was planning to open an office nearby. He confessed that some of the staff were prepared to move with him and in effect a mutiny was in the making. Practice owners are advised to be wary and ascertain the true intentions of their associate.

Obviously both the practice owner and the associate should adhere to fair business practices. Many young graduates are not ready for an ownership agreement because of their personal circumstances. Some will marry and start families and may not want to stay in a particular area. Ownership demands a commitment and a sense of permanence.

Associates who choose to accept an associate position are advised to seek an Associate Agreement. The agreement (see Appendix B for a sample copy) should not contain any mention of buying in or buying the practice outright. This would be premature for both parties. The Associate Agreement should be a contract focusing only on the employment conditions. Agreements to purchase should be negotiated at a later date, once compatibility has been determined and suitable timelines can be defined. This is typically a one- or two-year process.

Despite the importance of such agreements, research suggests that less than half of employer and associate relationships do not have a signed agreement in place. This is a recipe for disaster as either party could terminate the relationship at any time. This agreement should define many common practices. For example, associates typically feel entitled to contact the patients they have brought into the office, while practice owners often feel that such patients belong to the practice.

So who is correct? The provincial and state regulators have strict guidelines as to how and when dentists can contact patients for commercial purposes, but they normally do not intervene in commercial disputes. Thus, when departing dentists begin the fight over patients, an expensive lawsuit often results. A written agreement may have prevented this wasteful and often humiliating struggle. The authors' surveys show many dentists' friendships have been lost in this way.

CHAPTER 7

The Career Associate
and the Locum Dentist

The Career Associate

There are many very successful associate arrangements
whereby neither party wishes to be partners and the
junior is happy to remain as an associate for life.
Female dentists may seek this arrangement to allow
them the opportunity to raise a family. Most wish to
establish their own practice but often at a later time in
their career.

Locum Dentists — An Emerging Career Choice

The presence of the temporary dentist (the "temp") in
the workplace has become more and more commonplace. Often these dentists have sold their practices but
still wish to continue to practice, on a reduced schedule. Typically, these dentists have registered with a
locum service or independently freelance. A dentist

may also "temp" for the person who has bought his/her practice, when the purchaser takes vacations or temporary leaves for maternity, medical or other reasons. This makes perfect sense as patients and staff are most accepting of the former, and familiar, dentist. Production is usually maintained at similar levels, thus keeping the practice vibrant while the practice owner is off.

Medical doctors have been practising as locums for decades. Some associates never plan or want to own their own practice. They come and go as required, and are content to do so. Many previously retired dentists are now considering this as an alternative career choice due to the recent economic downturn.

The benefits of being a locum, much like those of an associate, are:

- *No financial commitment.*
- *Intermittent work* — You might work one or two months, then have one or two months off.
- *No burden of management* — The practice owner makes the decisions.
- *Freedom* — Some mature locums have limited family commitments and welcome the freedom to travel, pursue hobbies or live an alternative lifestyle.

The primary benefit of hiring a locum dentist is the ability to take a leave. Maternity leaves, due to the proliferation of female dentists, are about to increase substantially. Who will cover for these expectant mothers? Locums are needed! We have had several doctors keep their locum up to a year beyond what they were originally planning so they could enjoy their parenting time.

Baby boomer dentists (those who are now 40 to 60 years of age) are the majority of today's practitioners, and they are the most likely to experience a disability. Hundreds of interviews with dentists who are selling their practices reveal a large percentage are doing so because of a disability. The locum is the ideal source of interim labour to maintain patient care and assure the disabled dentist of income. Disability insurance will cover some of the expenses, but in most instances it is insufficient to maintain a full complement of staff. One client interviewed needed immediate surgery. The recovery period was estimated at one month. She chose to close the practice, temporarily lay off her staff, and notified the patients she would be back in a month. Her thinking was that very few, if any, patients would not be able to "wait for just one month to see me." Emergencies were referred to local congenial providers.

She suffered a relapse and notified her staff and patients about a further delay. Sadly, her health diminished further. She had already been closed for two months! Her short-term disability insurance was about to expire. A locum was found to carry on her practice. Luckily, after this two-month closure, none of the staff had found other employment and were willing to return. Only a handful of her patients had sought another dentist and the practice was back on track within weeks. This is a fortunate situation and it was possible only due to the lack of nearby competitors. The practice was situated in a smaller community and there were limited options for the patients to seek treatment elsewhere. In a larger city, where dentists are marketing for new patients much more assertively, this practice would have suffered a substantial loss of patients in this two-month period. Too often, dentists are overly optimistic about recovery from a disability.

Dentists are advised to protect their practice and hire a locum/freelance dentist or participate in a death and disability group. They can be called into service on short notice and relied upon until complete recovery occurs.

CHAPTER 8

The Preferred Model of Dental Practice: The Solo Dentist

Why Become a Dentist?

Informal surveys and research from lectures reveal that students choose dentistry for these four reasons:

1. They want to be their own boss.
2. A family member or relative is a dentist.
3. They like to work with their hands.
4. Dentistry is a lucrative profession.

In 1916, Clapp wrote that the economic objective in practice is this:

> *"Men practice dentistry to earn a living and a competency. This object has been so confused with the manner of such earning that it has often been lost sight of and violent discussions have raged about the methods employed, and left the principle untouched."*

What vision do young dentists have of their practices, if the first goal is to be their own boss? We suggest that vision be the model of the solo practice. Experience indicates this model works best for over 75% of North American dentists. The other 25% work within group practices, academia, public health services and professional consulting.

Why Then, Do Dentists Enter Group Practice?

Many dentists prefer to have a community of like-minded individuals who can help each other with the challenges of running the practice. They admit that they choose to be within a group for the perceived benefits of shared practice management roles. They believe that staff management, dealing with suppliers, dealing with landlords and other management issues would be best dealt with by a group.

While this has some merit, problems often arise as a result of the need for consensus within the group. Too many decision makers can be a dangerous formula. The following scenario illustrates this fact:

> *"Several years ago, I helped to manage the 13-chair 8-dentist office where I practiced. The financial returns were very respectable for this type of business. My accountant, however, had a different approach. He determined my net hourly income for my practice management duties. Then he compared it to my net hourly chair-side (patient treatment) income. The two were not even close! Patient treatment was far more lucrative than the time that I spent "running the practice." This very simple*

demonstration changed my direction and my profes-
sional focus."

This comes from the much-noted dental expert, Dr. George Freedman.

Further study into the history of leadership reveals this:

> *"A multitude of rulers is not a good thing, let there be one ruler, one king."*
> — HOMER

SETTING UP YOUR PRACTICE

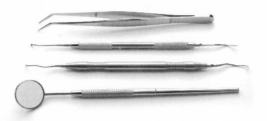

CHAPTER 9

Buying a Practice

. . . .

Who Should Set Up a New Practice?

The best candidates are those dentists without significant student debts, families or other financial obligations. Often they are living with parents or family and have ample free time to work evenings and weekends. Ideally, these candidates will purchase brand new equipment designed for a modern facility built to their personal specifications.

Patient flow may be scarce in the early years, and there may be long periods of downtime between patients. However, each new patient examination will be performed exactly as that dentist's unique philosophy dictates, and it is likely, with time, the practice will flourish. There will be a personal satisfaction that the practice succeeded because of the individual dentist's hard work, risk taking and decision making.

When Should a Dentist Buy a Practice?

Based on hundreds of interviews with young buyers, new graduates are likely to work in three to five different practices before reaching the stage when they are ready to buy. They may buy the practice they are working in, or another on the open market. In both cases, it will take time and patience to find the right practice. Too often, dentists buy the first practice offered to them and later admit they may have bought the wrong practice.

While young dentists must have patience in order to find their ideal practice, research suggests that dentists who purchase a practice at a younger age do financially better than those who wait.

When Is the Best Time to Buy a Dental Practice?

Buyers should be patient. Many factors come into play. A high level of clinical competency and confidence is required to start a solo practice. Secure financial backing has to be in place. Lenders will provide this only if the applying dentist is judged competent and has at least three to five years of experience.

Even if the above criteria are met, the right practice may not exist at the time. The location for a new office must be right. Competition is often fierce for an ideal office location. Landlords relate that they often have multiple bids for an office in a prime location. Successful established dental practices with a preferred office site can also have multiple offers, especially in the major cities.

Where Is the Best Place to Buy a Practice?

As of 2010, Jim Kasper Associates and ROI Corporation have examined the financial statements of over 12,000 dentists and this number will increase by about 500 dentists in each succeeding year.

In the year 2010, the top solo practitioner, as reported to Jim Kasper Associates, grossed in excess of $2.1 million and retained just over $1.3 million on an adjusted cash flow basis. This individual studied many other top performers to learn how to treat patients with the most extensive care, including implantology and various full mouth restoration techniques. Not every dentist will have the desire to be at this level, but it is achievable.

Naturally, the new patient flow and the nature of his patients contributed to his success and he could not have reached this level without possessing a certain level of charisma to gain the trust and confidence of his patients.

Some may be shocked to learn that this dentist is located in a rural town with six other dentists, situated one hour outside of a major New York city. At first glance, one may assume the patients, being rural people, could not possibly support these figures. The opposite appears to be true. These patients, having a more relaxed lifestyle, have more free time, ample ability to pay and can afford extensive treatments due to lower lifestyle costs. Some believe that big-city patients have more income, and this may be true, but with that comes increased living expenses and lifestyle habits.

Rural patients are very well informed of the need for dental care and often make ideal candidates for dentists to treat. They have a desire for increased cosmetics. Unfortunately, many of today's younger dentists fail to recognize this fact.

Data derived from JKA LLC and ROI Corporation appraisals suggest that the incomes of the rural dentists are increasing disproportionately compared to urban-based dentists. There are several reasons for this:

- The competition in rural areas is measurably lower.
- Overhead costs are lower as rents and wages average in the lower range.
- The patients have more free time and fewer demands for other lifestyle expenditures — housing is less costly and rural families tend to purchase fewer "conspicuous" items such as luxury cars and homes.

Despite these advantages, many young dentists interviewed report that they still want to set up practices in urban areas. They want to be near cultural centres, entertainment, friends and family. Many other factors, often personal and unique to the individual dentists, prevent them from venturing out to the rural areas. This is true in all states and Canadian provinces and it will probably remain this way for the foreseeable future as more and more females and ethnically diverse dentists enter the profession.

It's ironic that as the need for dentists increases in rural areas, there are fewer and fewer dentists seeking to locate there. The law of supply and demand will then dictate that the rural dentists, lacking in nearby competitors, will be able to increase their fees — within reason

— and can demand fees that are higher than those suggested by the dental associations. When combined with the lower overheads, this will result in even higher earnings for rural dentists. An abundance of patients will also allow them to eliminate advertising and other promotional costs, thus reducing overhead costs further.

As of 2015, it is likely that the typical rural dentist will have annual gross income exceeding one million dollars and that overheads will be no more than 50% of gross.

It would seem prudent for new dentists to closely examine the advantages inherent in a rural practice.

The Form of Ownership

In the U.S., tax law changes influence the entity selection of ownership. Most common are the 1120s — subchapter S corporation or the sole propietorship schedule "C." Not widely favored is the 1120 corporation or so-called C corp as it unfavorably taxes the owner when the practice is sold.

In Canada the ideal structure for owning a dental practice is a professional corporation. Only recently has this practice been allowed and now most dentists in Canada form a corporation and transfer their assets to that company. There are numerous benefits, including sharing of profits with family members (usually dividends) and the ability to sell your practice with greatly reduced income tax consequences.

As of 2007, each owner of a Canadian corporation is allowed up to $750,000 in tax-free capital gains for the sale of qualified shares in a corporation. When selling, it is advisable for dentists to incorporate, if they have not already done so. When buying a practice, the same advice is true — mostly for the ongoing tax benefits of distributing dividends to family and the ability to form an independent pension plan for the dentist.

There are many other reasons and exceptional circumstances that make incorporation beneficial. An accountant should always be consulted for tax matters.

Be patient, the right opportunity will come along eventually.

CHAPTER 10

Choosing and Setting Up
a New Practice

Until the 1970s, most graduating dentists would set up a new practice. Dentists were in short supply in many communities and patient flow was easy to develop. Many retired dentists relate that they simply signed a lease, bought some equipment and before their office door was opened they were booked for weeks. Today, this is a rare occurrence. The success of a new graduate setting up a practice is largely determined by office location and good fortune.

New Practices in Retail Locations

The trend towards retail dentistry began in the 1980s. Dr. Howard Rocket, one of the co-founders of Tridont Dental Centers, was a pioneer in bringing traditional dentistry to the retail environment. When asked why he did so, he responded:

"We saw potential because a great number of people were not getting dental treatments as dentists were rarely open evenings and weekends. We sought to deliver quality dentistry, at usual fees, during hours that were accessible and convenient to the public."

Locations with high visibility, signage and exposure to traffic flow became the preferred choice of many dentists. Dentists have located in newer medical professional buildings, shopping malls and retail plazas in the suburbs of all major cities. Once again, the demand for prime visible professional locations is high, and often the best offices are gone before the building opens.

Choosing to situate in shopping malls and retail plazas has some disadvantages:

- Rents are typically higher than in professional buildings.
- Retail demands evening and weekend hours, which may present a problem in the later stages of a dentist's career.
- Retail attracts good patient flow, but may also attract less reliable patients as retail tends to attract walk-ins — patients who are not always committed to optimal dental care, but only seeking immediate relief of an emergency.
- Building a practice in a retail plaza is more costly as landlords do not offer finished space and leasehold improvements will cost anywhere from $75 to $150 per square foot.

While retail practices are common in cities and suburban areas, many that have opened in the last five years are struggling. The existing dentists in the community are well established and while their location may be less visible than the newer retail locations, their reputation is the key reason their patients remain loyal to them.

New housing developments attract new patients, but the new homeowners already have a dentist somewhere, and the propensity for patients to remain loyal is very high in dental practice. Appraisals reveal that retail practices reach the break-even point in year two or three. How do young dentists manage to support themselves, service student debts (if applicable), pay the rent and wages, and service the bank loan required to build and equip the retail office?

The answer is likely that they fall deeper into debt while building their dream. This can be fatal to those who have not budgeted properly. (See Appendix G, Buy Versus Set-Up Comparison, for an example of an estimate of cash flow for the typical new retail practice.) It is evident that expenses exceed incomes for at least two years, on average.

Many of those who follow this path will work in other practices as an associate, waiting for their new practice to have enough patient flow. Lenders will require it. Patient flow may not be adequate to keep the new dentist busy, but by being absent he/she will be unaware of the opportunities to grow his/her practice each day.

New Practices in Non-Retail Locations

Professional buildings, renovated houses and office towers are just a few alternatives to retail locations. Today's dentists often think these are old-fashioned locales and not visible enough for patients to find them. This is not always true. Surveys reveal that the large majority of patients are attracted by referral, as opposed to location, advertising or promotions.

While many dentists continue to advertise using television, park benches, billboards, radio, direct mailings and other strategies, many older dentists reveal they wasted their hard-earned dollars on advertising when forming their practices. Research revealed that in one case a new dentist spent thousands on advertising as advised by his consultant. One year later his practice had grown by 30%. When his staff surveyed the patients as to why they chose that dental practice, over 80% replied that a friend referred them. The cost of the advertising was over $25,000! The number of new patients directly attributed to this expenditure was less than 50 (a cost of about $500 dollars per patient).

Advertising certainly can be beneficial and should not be ignored. Surveys reveal that satisfied patients provide the best "advertising" because of the high referral rate they provide.

Dental practices are no exception — referral is the best method of building a practice.

How do dentists ask for a referral from an existing patient? It's simple — just ask them! Many dentists have signs in their dental reception areas stating:

"The best compliment you can pay us is the referral of a family member or friend."

This excellent idea costs less than $50 and it works. However, not enough dentists go the extra step to reinforce the sign and actually ask for referrals. Some feel it is below their professional status to ask a patient to refer a friend. Others believe it may show weakness or give the impression they are not busy. This is erroneous thinking. Many businesses ask their clients for referrals. A typical request is as follows.

"If you are satisfied with the results please tell your colleagues about me."

Many clients accept this practice and consider it good business. Advertising and promotions have their place, but in the long run, it is this word-of-mouth referral upon which dental practices are built.

Ultimately, the non-retail location may be best for those who have the confidence and the charisma to ask for referrals. Shy dentists must rely upon non-verbal methods of attracting patients. This is appropriate and encouraged for those who are somewhat introverted. Psychological studies confirm that some dentists are just that — introverted. For them, retail may be the best option.

Other Factors

Those dentists who have a unique position because of religion, culture or ethnicity in the communities they serve should consider the non-retail location. Their ability to attract patients in relation to one or more of the above factors is enhanced. While this can be a clear advantage, it can also be a disadvantage. Sometimes they lose patients because of one or more of these factors. In addition, people of similar backgrounds often ask for and expect discounts. Research indicates that this is a common phenomenon to all ethnicities and cultures and may be a limiting factor with regard to profitability. There are many patients with limited incomes and financial pressures that deserve a break and this issue requires the dentist's best judgment.

Once the process of discounting dental fees is commenced, it will become a trademark of that practice.

Patients will tell others they can get a deal with this dentist and once the word is out, the result is a low-fee practice. Then, at some point, when the dentist attempts to establish a suitable price point for the location, the patients become upset and some will leave.

CHAPTER 11

The Size and Design of a New Dental Office

• •

There are many common mistakes made in the design of a dental office. The first is that the dentist rented too much space. Landlords have a vested interest in renting out larger offices. Dental equipment dealers also recommend larger offices as this allows for future equipment purchases. A single dentist should be able to operate effectively in an office of 1,350 to 1,800 square feet, with three to four operatories. Start up loans are usually 30% hard costs (cabinetry and equipment) and 70% soft costs (construction, working capital and supplies). Prudent dentists will sign a lease that falls within this size.

There are many examples of dental practices working profitably and effectively in 1,200 square feet, with three operatories and a compact design. In fact, there are examples of two–operatory practices occupying approximately 450 square feet that are elegant, efficient and profitable.

The temptation to oversize arises from a perceived need for privacy, staff rooms and storage, and to accommodate patient traffic flow. These are very important matters when designing the new office. The dentist's private office should be kept to a bare minimum.

"Dentists spend money when they're in the private office — they make money when they're in the operatory."
— ROY BROWN

Dr. John Wilson, who has worked as a locum dentist in dozens of dental offices, believes that most offices lack an intelligent ergonomic design. He reports that the operator's chair, the location of instrumentation and the lighting are inadequate in most operatories. In many practices he has found that the operatory countertops are cluttered with unused equipment.

According to Dr. Wilson, many dentists like to buy expensive high-tech gadgets that take up space and often do not generate additional income. Some devices may speed delivery of care, yet others only change the form of delivery. Dentists should choose their tools carefully and conservatively. Many of the new tools and technologies should only be purchased after their worth has been proven and the practice warrants their need and is able to support them.

Roy Brown's studies with Wilson Southam from The Group at Cox Company have proven invaluable in office design. They performed "time in motion" studies of dentists at work. They filmed them for several days in order to identify inefficiencies. Then, by accident, an important observation was made when the film of the dentists working was sped up. In high speed the wasted motions and hand actions of the dentists were revealed. It was discovered that much of the dentists' time was used for repetitive motions, many of which were damaging to the dentists' hands, arms, neck and back. This finding led to the four-handed revolution (dentist and assistant) in dentistry and raised a question about office size.

What's the Right-Sized Office?

In a typical solo practice the staff consists of one full-time dental assistant, a receptionist and a hygienist. In most instances, a typical office will host a maximum of three staff, along with the dentist and two or three patients. The total number of people in a solo practice, even with family members waiting and other visitors, is usually no more than eight to ten people. An industry norm for office space design and allocation of person space is 100 to 200 square feet per person.

The typical dental operatory is about 100 to 150 square feet. Therefore, for a three-operatory practice, no more than 450 square feet per operatory, which would include common areas.

When you consider that three people are usually in the dentist's operatory (the dentist, assistant and patient), and the hygienist and one patient are in another, you have five people in less than 300 square feet.

The balance of the person space is for the receptionist and those waiting. When asked why she had only two chairs and a small magazine rack in her waiting room of less than 100 square feet, a dentist responded:

"Good dentists don't keep their patients waiting, so two chairs is all I need."

By following the above advice, the savings (due to the decreased rent paid) would approximate $100,000 over a 25-year period.

While sterilization and storage areas are essential, they rarely occupy someone for more than a few minutes at a time. Hence, these areas should be compact and efficient. Storage is an issue for most paper-based businesses. In order to save space and rent, dentists should regularly cull their files of inactive patients. Most offices now use electronic files with a suitable electronic backup to help eliminate paper record storage.

Dave Love, who works with Patterson Dental Canada, one of the largest suppliers of dental equipment in North America, says this about dental office design:

"Most dentists do not plan for enough storage and function within their offices. There are many experts to help with your design . . . use them, they've been there before."

The modern business office must accommodate an electronic workstation. Older office designs did not foresee the need for computers, monitors, printers and the like, as well as the cabling required. Modern computer furniture is ergonomically designed and hides most of the unsightly cabling. The new office must take advantage and be aware of the cutting edge furniture available.

Record Storage

The trend towards 8.5" by 12" file folders will likely continue for quite a while until all practices become fully computerized. These files hold panoramic x-rays and the many other documents required for the present standard of record keeping. The typical office design should allow the receptionist easy access to the files without the files necessarily being fully visible to patients. Cabinets with doors should be used to ensure patient confidentiality and compliance with HIPPA.

As a practice grows, files accumulate and many become worn. With the modern computer software available, some of the storage problems may be eliminated. In the U.S. it is likely that paper records will continue to be the standard for at least another 10 to 20 years — thus the new dental office design should contain a concealed and private file chart and records room adjacent to the reception area. Conversion to patient electronic medical records is expected by 2015 and for practices with high volume medicaid patients it will be mandated. However, practices who have low volume Medicaid patients will not be mandated to convert, but may receive lower reimbursements.

The Private Office and Staff Room

Dental office staff will need a private space to retire to for lunch and breaks. This room is often neglected in office design. It should be compact, yet comfortable and easy to keep clean and tidy. It should contain a sink, a fridge, a microwave and provisions for making tea and coffee, along with a place to sit. Providing these basics indicates the dentist's concern for the needs of his/her staff and respects their need for a private space and private time.

The dentist's own private office should be small and compact in order to keep within the overall 1,200± square foot office design. Time must be spent to keep this office organized and tidy. Any financial, personal or confidential papers should be under lock and key. These should be eventually removed and stored in a more secure location.

Patient interviews reveal that many patients' opinions of the dentist are based on the overall appearance and cleanliness of all aspects of the practice. They are often unaware of the strict sterilization protocols, but remember the clutter in the waiting room. They appreciate that the dentist's and the staff's credentials, educational degrees and achievements are displayed in easy view but not to excess. They can often recall any artwork that was on display.

The Waiting Room

The waiting room should have a comfortable place to wait that does not allow the patient to overhear phone conversations or the receptionist's discussions with other patients. Some current magazines and a small area with books and toys that would interest children are a nice touch. In the unlikely event that the dentist is running late, a clock should not be visible in the waiting room to avoid staff or patient stress.

The Treatment Planning Room

This room is solely for discussing complex cases and financial matters. It is essential, but again, should only be large enough to accommodate three people at a time. This allows for the person giving the treatment (not always the dentist), the patient and one family member to go over all aspects of the treatment.

Specialists, such as orthodontists, typically require larger rooms for presenting treatments. This room should be free of all clinical materials and be non-threatening in all regards. Ideally, the room should be elegant in its simplicity. Some dentists prefer to post their degrees here in order to ensure their patients know they are qualified.

Washrooms

Ideally, two bathrooms within your dental suite are best, one for patients and one for staff. Many landlords of older, existing buildings are not able to provide two bathrooms within a suite. If you are fortunate enough to secure a lease prior to final construction, then plan to install two bathrooms. Toothbrushes, mouthwash and cups are a welcome addition for patient use before treatment.

With many of the above considerations in mind, a

dentist should be able to design an office that meets the criteria and remains within a 1,200± square foot limitation. In doing so, he or she will maximize profitability while providing for the comfort and needs of patients and staff.

Maintaining Your Dental Office

Dentists are well trained to maintain a sterile clinical space but often their front office does not project the image of cleanliness. The front of a dental practice is like a show room. It must always be clean, uncluttered and welcoming to patients. This is an opportunity to impress them. Many patients own their own businesses and may judge your clinical skills according to your office cleanliness and organization.

Once in the clinical areas, patients will notice any faults or eyesores — even in areas such as the ceiling! Dentists should sit in their patient chairs and observe what their patients are seeing. Often the ventilation ducts are dirty and ceiling tiles have unsightly water stains from condensation from the overhead pipes.

Most office cleaners are not given enough time to adequately clean an office. The typical dentist will hire a firm to clean once a week. In doing so, the cleaners are given three or four hours to perform a series of routine tasks — the floors, bathrooms and counter tops — basically they look down while they clean. Rarely do they look up or think to dust where patients look. Set out a specific, alternating cleaning schedule of specific areas for them. This may increase your weekly fees but it is worth it.

CHAPTER 12

Financing a New or Established Practice

All major North American banks and specialty practice lenders are interested in financing dentists. They know that a dental practice is a wise investment and regularly provide term loans and lines of credit to get them started. When starting up a new practice they sometimes ask for additional security, over and above the equipment and leaseholds, to secure their loan.

Leasing companies also provide financing for start-up, typically at slightly higher interest rates. Most leasing companies do not offer lines of credit for initial operating costs; thus new dentists often seek a line of credit from a bank or specialty practice lender.

Leasing allows for accelerated tax deductions, versus the traditional method of depreciating equipment over longer periods of time.

Buying an Established Practice

The specialty practice lenders are the best choice for the purchase of a practice with existing cash flow. They usually offer competitive interest rates and expedient service. A sample loan proposal can be obtained from almost any lender. Since an established practice has a proven track record, you can usually negotiate more favourable terms with the lender as compared to financing a new start-up.

While very few dentists actually declare bankruptcy each year (the rate of bankruptcy for dentists is well below the norm for other businesses), banks are conservative by nature and often request a complete business plan for the new start-up loan application. This plan takes considerable work, as it must be well documented and supported by competition overviews and a demographic analysis of the planned location.

A young dentist, interviewed a few years ago, prepared an elaborate business plan based on extensive research, and successfully obtained a bank loan to set up a brand new retail dental office. He opened up a beautiful new office within nine months, proudly inviting many guests to the opening ceremony. The office was modern, well designed and situated in a high-growth area.

The office had room for five operatories that he chose to fully equip from the beginning. Although he knew that he did not have enough patients to justify equipping five operatories, the price was favourable because he was buying in quantity. Unfortunately, his growth was a little slower than budgeted, and the loan payments, when combined with high rent (due to the high-profile retail location he selected) and staff wages, exceeded the monthly cash flow for the first few years.

Fortunately, he did not have large personal debts, as he was single and living at home with parents. To make ends meet he began working as an associate in another office. His absence from his own practice at this crucial time of development further aggravated his problems.

The lesson here is obvious — do not borrow too much too soon. New practices require constant attention and full-time attendance. A new practice should start with one or two fully equipped operatories. As the practice grows and cash flow increases, new operatories can be added. New dentists should resist the temptation to secure discounts for bulk purchases.

CHAPTER 13

Buying an Established Practice, and Clinical Compatibility

. . . .

Who Should Buy a Practice?

The ability to secure a list of patients is the primary reason to buy a practice. Dentists with large student loans, families, mortgages and other debts should seriously consider associating for a longer period, or they should investigate the purchase of an established practice with existing cash flow. Some argue that delaying ownership conflicts with their desire to be their own boss. The delay is unavoidable for some, often for financial reasons. Others feel that if they buy a practice they will not have the new equipment and décor they desire. The cosmetic elements of a practice are easily modified over time.

One compromise is that the philosophy of the previous owner is well entrenched in the minds of the staff and patients, and a sudden change can be upsetting. When buying a practice, dentists should consider the following:

Make as few major changes as possible for the first year.

Once the dentist has introduced him/herself to the patients and met with them at least twice, they will be relatively comfortable with the dentist. This usually takes about two recall appointments, or about one year. At this point, the cash flow will be consistent, and any modifications the dentist wishes to implement will be more easily accepted and should be more affordable.

For dentists purchasing an established practice, the most important consideration is to find an office where the clinical philosophy is similar to their own. Two like-minded dentists will easily transition a practice from one to the other.

How Do You Determine Clinical Compatibility?

Most dental practices for sale do not allow the prospective buyers to work in the office prior to an offer having been made. Owners want to keep the sale of their practice confidential. If more than one prospective buyer is allowed to "test drive" the practice, confusion for both patients and staff results, and invariably production drops when the "test driver" leaves.

Owners are certainly not interested in losing income as the prospective buyer makes up his/her mind. There are consultants who promote the "hire your buyer" theory, which means that the most serious candidate is allowed to work in the practice prior to making their offer. This has merit, but mostly benefits the buyer. The owner is kept in a state of anxiety while the young, less-experienced dentist examines every aspect of the practice. Often, this can generate negative side effects that can damage the goodwill value of a practice. In the end, it is best to avoid hiring the prospective buyer as preconditional to the sale.

How Do You Determine Whether a Practice Matches Your Clinical Philosophy if You Cannot See Patients and Work with the Staff?

This can be ascertained by examining the following:

- *The method of scheduling* — How much time is being allotted for various procedures reveals the style and skills of the dentist and the practice's main sources of income.
- *The equipment, supplies and materials used* — The technique of one dentist is easily determined when another examines their instruments, materials and operatory set up.
- *The overall décor and layout of the office* — A thorough inspection of all the facilities often reveals much about the personality of the selling dentist and the overall makeup of the practice.

While the above considerations may seem obtuse, it is important to remember that in the past dentists often never met until an offer was agreed upon. Today, most qualified buyers are permitted the opportunity to meet the owner and make an initial examination of the premises before making an offer.

The practice of keeping the buyer uninformed about the staff and patients is in place for a reason — you are buying a business, not people. Although the list is the business asset that is being sold, meeting the patients does not alter the view of most buyers, as they admit that they simply want a pool of patients to treat.

Other characteristics of the patients are easily determined with the aid of modern computers. The ethnicity is easily found by examining charts that contain last names. Most computer systems can also generate geographic profiles: for example, where the patients come from. Some can even prepare insured-versus-uninsured patient reports and average patient age.

It is much easier today for an owner to educate a buyer about his/her practice. Buyers can be confident that they will be able to determine the style and modalities of practice, and, most importantly, the clinical philosophy of the owner without the need to meet the staff or to work in the practice.

Strategies for Managing Staff

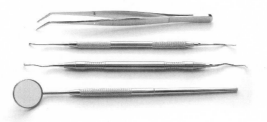

CHAPTER 14

Running a
Dental Practice

● ●

The greatest management challenge dentists face is managing people. Staff, patients, suppliers and lab technicians can be the most demanding and unpredictable part of a day, yet they are the most critical element of the business. Dentists relate that they are well trained to provide dental care but often struggle with their people skills.

How Can Dentists Develop Their People Skills?

Older dentists relate that these skills are developed with time, trial and error. Once in practice, they were faced with handling numerous daily tasks influenced by people's fears, objections, emotions and perceived needs. Many dentists relate that dealing with their staff is even more difficult than handling their patients. There are individual differences in the staff-dentist relationships, as well as in inter-staff relationships. Both have to be overseen by the dentist.

Interviews reveal that most dentists have not written or purchased an office policy manual. They admit that they rely on advice gathered informally from their colleagues and third-party advisors. There are many well-conceived office manuals available, yet few dentists believe these standard references are appropriate for their unique style of management.

Dentists who do not have an office manual, whether purchased or self-written, do so at their own peril. The manual provides a starting point for both the dentist and his/her staff. It can avoid many potential problems and expedite many that arise.

The manual should be an ever-changing document that is modified as time goes by and good business practices change. Staff should be reminded regularly of office policies and updated on all changes made.

Associates should learn from their employer's successes or failures, and develop their own unique model. Once in ownership, new ideas can be tried and their outcomes analyzed in order to build a manual that works. Templates for dental practice manuals are available and many courses are offered that provide guidelines. Over time, an office manual will become an integral part of the dentist's practice and reflect the needs of the dentist, staff and patients.

More on Staff Relations

Dentist interviews reveal this common query:
"What if they don't like me?"

While being liked by staff is important, it should not be an obsession, and many dentists miscalculate what their relationship with their staff should be. The staff's first priority is to be employed in a job for which they are trained and suitably qualified. Secondly, and not to be underestimated, is that all employees want to work in an environment where they feel needed and are respected by all other people in the workplace.

In many cases the staff are somewhat indifferent to the owner, as long as they have learned to get along with him/her. It is often the other staff that cause the unsettling moments of tension within the office.

Assembling a team of like-minded individuals who trust and respect each other is of greater importance than hiring staff that like the dentist.

Many speakers on staff relations talk and write about people working in harmony toward a higher and often lofty goal. This is an excellent concept and one that people should strive for. The reality is that staff are more often there for income and security reasons, rather than the contrived ideals of management experts.

Dentists should respect and reward their staff for their work performance. They should be kind and thoughtful employers, but they should not attempt to be their employees' best friend.

In 1916, Clapp wrote:

"A most disagreeable feature of young lady assistants is that many of them regard 'the job' as merely a stepping stone from school to the altar."

While this is dated, and somewhat chauvinistic, it still holds true to some extent for people of both genders. Working in a dental office is temporary for some, and they have little intention of remaining in the practice as a career choice. Many of today's assistants aspire to be hygienists or to move on to other pursuits. Dentists would be wise to understand this.

Hiring simplified — hire candidates with great attitudes. Always hire slowly and fire quickly.

CHAPTER 15

Selecting a Business System

How do you run a dental practice? Business systems are the tools of managing the flow of information. Today, computers perform most of the functions, yet people are the ones who enter and manage the data.

Modern software has an incredible capability to deliver crucial data. One mistake made by many dentists is that they do not understand their software and leave this task to their staff. In doing so dentists are in danger of losing control that may lead to employee misappropriation of money. Fraud is evident in all businesses, and dentistry is no exception. There are courses that can be taken to help identify and prevent fraud, but the central problem is that the dentist does not understand the software system or how to control cash flow. It is very easy to alter entries and delete charges once a patient has paid.

A recent case involved a dentist who was the victim of theft exceeding $200,000. He had a very loyal receptionist who always looked after all his finances — both business and personal. She had systematically stolen small amounts daily for over 15 years.

She was able to pull this off for years until a new banker at his branch performed a random review of several clients' depositing practices. In an attempt to reduce the dentist's monthly bank fees, his banker noticed dual accounts — one for the dentist, one for her. At first he was furious, then he felt humiliated and sank into a mild depression. How could she do that to him after all those years? She was relieved of her position and he had no choice but to prosecute. A small amount was recovered and he is still in practice, but he claims he still feels demoralized.

The lesson to be learned for dentists is not to be overly trusting. One person should never be allowed to control business and personal finances and to perform all the tasks of billing, collecting, depositing and managing the practice's funds.

Many dentists employ a spouse or family member to supervise this essential aspect of business ownership. Others use a third party, a bookkeeper who is only involved in preparing payables and financial reports.

One key indicator that staff members may be committing fraud is that they refuse to take vacations. They must remain on the job constantly to keep their system of fraud concealed. If you have a staff member, who handles billing or collections and he/she never takes a vacation, be warned.

CHAPTER 16

Staff Wages and Bonus Systems

Dentists have employed many types of bonus systems as incentives for staff to reach higher levels of performance. A bonus system is a great idea and experience suggests the following:

- Bonuses should be random.
- Bonuses should be immeasurable by staff.

They should never be tied to specific dates, events, anniversaries or factors that lead a staff member to conclude that they are more or less automatic.

One exception that seems to prevail for many is a bonus at Eid, Hanukkah or Christmas time. Another exception to the rule occurs when a long-standing tradition has been established in the practice that would be both difficult and unwise to eliminate.

Staff should be apprised when business is good but not be made aware of all financial statements. Performance bonuses should be paid on a random, ever-changing timetable. When bonuses are distributed, all that needs to be said is as follows:

"Lately we have done well, thank you for a job well done!"

In this way, the dentist remains in control of the bonus system. The bonus amount can and probably should vary from employee to employee. Staff members are unique and so are their levels of effectiveness, contribution and seniority. As much as possible, each bonus should be kept confidential to avoid staff jealousy and unnecessary questioning about the rationale for bonus amounts.

Initially, there is little that can be done if staff members choose to reveal their earnings and/or the amount of their bonuses. If this becomes problematic, then staff should be confronted individually and made aware of office policies that discourage sharing such information. If need be, justification for such policies should be made on the basis that only the dentist has all the facts necessary to make determinations on wages and bonuses.

Many experts and dentists argue for a system that is more transparent. Some offices actually post daily, weekly and monthly income information in a staff room. Staff become aware of income statements, wages paid and bonuses given. The belief is that by having all information available to everyone, productivity will increase.

Experience has shown that the transparent model is more likely to lead to unnecessary and counter-productive questioning of the dentist's rationale and decision-making skills. In addition, greed, jealousy and resentment are often by-products.

Dentists are advised to keep their financial state-ments private for the most part. Some statistics should be shared with staff, such as total patients seen in a day, or the occasional monthly objective, such as keeping collections to a certain level of production. This is a good business practice because it is inclusive just as it is necessary to inform staff when things are not up to the dentist's standards.

Some Pitfalls to Avoid

One dentist interviewed revealed that his staff knew everything because of the records on the office com-puter. He was asked the following:

"Do your staff know all of the expenses of your practice?"

He readily admitted that they did not, and he also went on to say that he was earning much less than his staff thought. He was embarrassed to tell his staff how high the overhead was, and he wanted to maintain the image of a successful dentist. This position, while hon-ourable, left him to pay higher wages than the industry norm.

He was advised by a consultant that staff should

cost between 28% and 32% of total billings — so he always paid wages and bonuses that equalled that amount by the end of the year. Staff cost analysis revealed he was paying substantially higher wages.

The lesson here is that guidelines and consultant advice can be misleading. Dentists should pay what is fair for their area and their marketplace.

One dentist made a habit of hiring young, inexperienced people for low wages. He took great time to train them and to teach them his methods of running a dental practice. His total wages, when divided into his gross income, were 11%. If he had used the guideline of the consultants, he would have paid out another 20% of his gross income just to be in line with industry averages. The competency of such workers was not a question as they were well trained. In return, they were paid on time, and understood and enjoyed their position in the practice.

The highest wages, as a percentage of gross, are usually found in the newer practices, and most often in the new start-up practice. When gross is small due to limited patient flow, wages can be as much as 50% of billings. When all remaining expenses are paid, the owners discover they have subsidized the practice for one or two years. Once a practice has surpassed the break-even point, wages should fall in line with the U.S. industry norm of 24% to 29% of gross including payroll taxes. (See Appendix G, Buy Versus Set-Up Comparison.) There will always be exceptions, and one or two percentage points should not measure success. The key to remember is that practices can be run on low wages as long as staff are well trained and those wages are viable in the marketplace in which the practice is run. Dental associations, dental study clubs, appraisers and consultants often make this information available for a fee.

One client indicated that his bonus system was based on the number of new patient exams performed each month. He set a base number of 25 new exams per month; each one thereafter earned a specified amount that was pooled and distributed to staff at the end of the month, based on seniority. This sounds simple enough. However, he was distraught to learn that for many years several of the staff had been booking phantom patients into the system to increase the numbers. The dentist was a kind, trusting man, and given his busy schedule and personal obligations, he never went back each month to verify that the new patient exams were actually performed. He trusted the computer reports and his staff. He had paid out bonuses (most of which were legitimately payable to the staff) in excess of $25,000. In particular, he noticed that the receptionist had entered many false names to increase her bonus by $100 per month. Had he made the bonus system random and immeasurable, this would not have occurred.

CHAPTER 17

Benefits and Performance Reviews

Other than the mandatory payment of CPP, social security and unemployment insurance and mandatory holiday pay (if offered), most dentists do not offer benefits. Since most staff are female, it is assumed they are married or will marry and have a spouse who has a full-time position with family benefits. Many are young and require little in terms of health care benefits at this early stage of their life. As they mature, their need for benefits will increase, and some dentists then offer benefits such as free dental care for them and their families, a contribution to the pension and profitsharing (IRA) or even a structured and defined benefits package for the entire staff.

It is an individual choice to offer benefits. Experience indicates that paying a slightly higher wage is just as effective as a benefits package. The best benefit you can offer staff is a higher wage for a job well done! They can spend it as they see fit.

Performance Reviews

"An order that can be misunderstood will be misunderstood."
— NAPOLEON BONAPARTE

When assessing performance, dentists are reminded that they are responsible for the direction given to staff. Staff can only perform as instructed or as requested, and rarely will they exceed expectations — it's the nature of the employee mentality.

Most business owners dread the annual review process. It is an old custom that has merit, but it causes the staff and the owner anxiety. Research suggests the best way to review the performance of a staff member is the continuous method. When someone performs well, let them know — recognition is one of the top three reasons people enjoy their jobs.

When employees perform poorly, inform them immediately. There is no advantage in waiting. A clear, gentle suggestion as to expectations is required; then move on. When employment anniversaries arrive, you can offer staff an increase in wage without the stressful review of the past mistakes. Successful dentists rarely hold a meeting with a staff member on his/her anniversary to review shortcomings; they mostly want to reward staff for another year of loyalty and to offer them an increase in wage.

How Much Should You Increase Wages?

Wages are an important measurement of an individual's "worth" in the market. Once a starting wage is established most employees will expect an increase each year. In the U.S. most dentists will look at the Consumer Price Index (CPI) to formulate a staff payrate increase. The Bureau of Labor Statistics has great information on wage rates by area and occupation (www.bls.gov/bls/blswage.htm). Their site is a useful tool that may assist the practice owner with appropriate pay scales for each staff member.

In Canada, most dentists will follow the cost of living index as published by the Government of Canada (www.statcan.gc.ca). There are ample references to cost of living indexes on the Internet. They measure the effective increase in the costs of running a household for the average Canadian. Unfortunately, if this is the only increase given, it does not reward for increased performance or seniority. This only allows an increase for the Cost of Living Allowance (COLA). Our research suggests adding 1% or 2% to the COLA is fair.

Wages should increase by no more than 3% in a stable economy, and perhaps marginally lower in times of low inflation. After 5, 10 or 15 years, many dentists offer additional bonuses for seniority such as additional vacation pay.

CHAPTER 18

Personnel Manuals, Office Policy and Staff Dismissal

Should staff be asked to sign an office policy acknowledgement? When hiring a new staff member, the answer is Yes. In addition some states mandate that written notice of pay, payday and location of payment be signed by all employees. Each staff member should be given a copy of the office policies and their employment duties, and each employee should sign a copy of the documents. Go to individual state employment compliance departments for information on these important documents.

The most contentious issue arising in the modern dental practice is the non-solicitation clause. Essentially, this clause restricts an employee from contacting patients in the event he/she quits or is dismissed from a practice. Hygienists have the greatest influence in this regard and many dentists are concerned that they may attract patients to a nearby competitor. The hygienist has more contact with patients than the dentist in many instances and often develops a stronger relationship with the patients.

When hiring a new hygienist, it is unreasonable to ask her/him to sign a contract. For existing hygienists in the practice, asking them to sign a contract with a non-solicitation clause will cause them to fear for the security of their position — they will assume that dismissal is pending. While this may not be the dentist's intention, it will likely be the perception of a long-standing staff member. Several states have well-defined right to work laws and restrictive covenants or contracts are not enforceable.

Dismissing a Staff Member

Many dentists and business owners tell of the trauma they experienced when letting staff go. This is probably one of the most difficult tasks dentists have to do.

Some words of advice:

- Obtain proper advice from an employment specialist — usually a lawyer.
- Document everything!
- Do it sooner rather than later!

Rarely does a bad employment situation get better. Many business owners feel obligated toward their employees. They often feel guilty. Dentists must remember that they have obligations to their own practice, their staff, their family and the industry as a whole. In these matters it is essential to act with decency and to be gentle but firm.

Dentists should record every event that has transpired. This gives them the rationale for dismissing a staff member. These records should indicate the actions that reveal the employee's incompetence or that is contrary to office policies and job descriptions.

One dentist related that he was unaware of the actions a staff member was taking because he did not work directly with her. She had been openly criticizing other staff in the presence of the patients. It was discovered when a close friend who was also a patient finally told the dentist that his long-term staff member was making derogatory racial remarks about another staff member. This was unacceptable, and he was forced to dismiss her. Unfortunately, he had no proof, as the other staff members would not admit to or verify the racial slurs — likely for fear of the repercussions. He chose not to mention the racial issue when dismissing her, using the poorly disguised excuse that she was not performing her tasks adequately. The problem was that she was actually very good at her job. After being released, she sought the advice of a labour law specialist who informed her that she had been wrongfully dismissed, whereby she sued the dentist. He never gave any evidence about the true reason she was dismissed, and he lost the case, resulting in a payment to her of almost one year's wages. The message here is to document everything, record the facts, obtain staff testimonials (where possible) and act decisively.

CHAPTER 19

Workplace Harassment and Staff Training

· ·

Unfortunately, there are instances where the dentist may be responsible for some form of harassment of the staff. Dentistry can be stressful, and on occasion dentists vent their frustrations on the staff. This can be prevented by recognizing that staff are one of the greatest influences on the overall business performance. In many instances, harassment issues can be avoided by stepping back and taking a long, sober pause. Things often look different after a good night's sleep.

Dentists should, at all costs, avoid romantic involvement with their staff. Office romances between staff should also be contrary to office policy. After becoming aware of a romantic entanglement, one dentist claims to have given the following advice:

> "I'm from a fishing village and we have a saying there: 'Don't fish off your own wharf.'"

From the early 1900s to the 1960s, the large majority of dentists were male, and the majority of staff were, and still are, female. Given the close proximity in which dentists and their staff work, it is understandable that romances sometimes result. Often these take the form of an extramarital affair.

The most costly business decision you will ever make is to have an office affair — especially if you're married!

ROI Corporation has been retained to perform hundreds of appraisals as a result of matrimonial breakdown. In some instances, the office romance was the reason for the divorce. The effects on the business are often disastrous. Office tensions soar as a result of the changed dynamics, and business invariably suffers, at least for a time. While many of these romances do lead to long-term successful relationships, it is strongly recommended that dentists avoid them.

Staff Training

Most dentists pay for staff to attend industry conventions and seminars. Their wages are paid for the time spent, and course fees are usually paid as well. Others pay only the wage, and ask the staff to pay for the continuing education — a practice that is unfair and leads to resentment. If staff are sent to a course or convention, even if it's deemed to be "fun," they should be paid both their wages and all other related costs, with the exception of meals.

There are many courses offered by a wide variety of

experts on staff morale, office functionality, increasing performance and other important topics. Both dentists and staff should attend these regularly. One client sent his entire team to a highly respected program promising to increase income and profitability of the practice. He did not attend. When the staff returned, they were full of new ideas and concepts that they wanted to implement. He allowed them to proceed, only to discover that the tactics were not in keeping with his philosophy. Yes, the methods employed were being used in other dental offices, and they did indeed increase production — but at what cost?

The assertive tactics of the staff offended some long-standing patients, as they suggested that more dentistry was needed than the dentist had recommended. The experts had told the staff about a treatment planning method that would persuade patients to accept more treatments. Staff want to be on a winning team, one that succeeds and that will eventually be able to afford to pay higher wages. However, dentists should be very careful about the courses they send staff to, and should attend with them to be sure what they are learning is consistent with the dentist's overall philosophy.

Optimizing Success

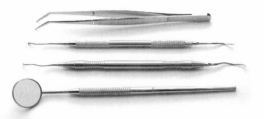

CHAPTER 20

Secrets of a Successful Practice

The top three secrets to success in dental practice are:

1. Be patient-focused first and foremost.
2. Respect and recognize your staff.
3. Do not be afraid to say "no thank you" to sales people if you are not clear about the benefits of their products.

Patients are the only source of income for the practice. They should be cared for in a fashion that reflects appreciation of their trust and confidence. As previously discussed, many dentists have difficulty relating to and conversing with their patients. Dentists must make every effort to develop people and conversational skills in order to have a genuine relationship with patients. This may require attendance at seminars designed for this purpose and a constant awareness of this personal need.

Why Do Patients Remain Loyal to Their Dental Office?

There are five key reasons patients return to your practice (in order of importance):

1. *Location* — proximity to work or home
2. *Staff* — familiar and friendly people
3. *Policies* — patients know what to expect
4. *The Dentist* — a trusted source of care
5. *Habit* — people do not like change, particularly with health care providers

While many argue that patients return primarily for the dentist, research suggests that this is the fourth most important reason. There are thousands of cases on record where dentists have been successively replaced by new, and often younger, dentists.

What Happens When There Is a Change in Dentist?

The authors' surveys indicate the two key statistics that prevail every time a dental practice is sold:

1. 85% to 95% of the patients return within a year, even when their dentist of many years retires.
2. Revenues increase 5% to 15% within one year.

This would suggest that while there are many loyalties to a dental practice, these are not necessarily attributed to the dentist.

Why Does the Income Go Up Within the First Year?

Young dentists are determined to repay student or

bank loans. They tend to take less time off than the previous dentist. They also bring new ideas, energy and drive to the practice. They are highly motivated and will almost always outperform the previous dentist. The new dynamic and the energy flow created are reflected in staff revitalization and patient curiosity to meet the new dentist. There is a new buzz in the practice, and increased production is often the result.

The new dentist is often trained in procedures that were previously referred out. Many of today's young buyers with three to five years of experience have taken courses in endodontics, orthodontics and implant surgery. While they are still relatively new to the profession, many are more than capable, and with the aid of modern tools and techniques, they are performing a wider array of treatments compared to the last generation of general dentists. This increases production substantially in some instances.

One practice examined was performing only the regular recall appointments and simple restorative work. The dentist was capable; he just did not like the long appointments and the stress of surgery or complicated dentistry. He was referring out all his endodontics, surgery, orthodontics and even some crown and bridge work — the favorite of most dentists. He admitted that he was very conservative and many of his patients were in need of extensive treatments. Within one year of a new dentist taking over, revenues almost doubled from $600,000 to well over $1,000,000!

The new owner related that she found the transition very easy since patients actually wanted more extensive treatments, but mentioned that they did not want to question the judgment of or to insult their former dentist by suggesting he was not meeting their needs. Most patients are very understanding and trust their dentist. In today's society, patients are demanding a wider scope of options from their dentist.

The proliferation of cosmetics, mostly for baby boomers, is a dentist's dream come true. Witness the TV shows that promote complete makeovers and you will see that cosmetic dental enhancement is almost always part of the process. This trend, while appearing to be superficial or temporary, is likely to last for at least another 20 years while the boomer generation continues to improve their physical appearance.

Managing Your Overhead

The top four expenses in every dental practice are:

1. Wages
2. Supplies
3. Laboratory
4. Rent

For solo dental practices, the average portion of total revenue spent is:

1. Wages — 24% to 29%
2. Supplies — 5% to 8%
3. Lab — 6% to 10%
4. Rent — 3% to 6%

Much has been said about keeping costs in check, and the best-run practices track their monthly and annual expenses with ease. Cash flow analysis and control is not as difficult as some believe; it's simply the art of recording the expenses, tracking them over specified time periods and measuring the results against the trend in total income.

There are many systems for charting your individual expenses, usually with the aid of a spreadsheet program such as Microsoft Excel, and with regular input, the top four expenses can be monitored.

Dentists often turn to third parties for help with the task of understanding their overhead (more often than is necessary at times). Experts who analyze financial statements are readily available, but many dentists perform their own analysis and believe it allows them better control of their finances

CHAPTER 21

Advertising and Income Hours in the Dental Practice

In the early 1980s, a challenge was made to the rules governing dental professionals' advertising tactics. Until then, most regulatory bodies permitted a dentist to post signs of no more than four inches in height, and the practice of advertising was strictly controlled and even classified as "professional misconduct" by some. After a lengthy battle, the courts ruled that dentists should be allowed to advertise much like traditional business owners. The gates had been opened, and all forms of advertising and promotion ensued.

A glance at today's telephone directories and Internet health professional listings reveal a major trend toward aggressive marketing. Dentists are using sophisticated and effective color ads to promote their practices.

As well, in every major city, dentists can be seen advertising on roadside billboards, park benches, neon signs, radio, TV and other media. Dentists have been forced to be more creative and have used a variety of promotions to set themselves apart from the rest of the competition.

One client related that he spends over $20,000 per month on various forms of advertising, resulting in a higher than average new patient flow. He went on to suggest that many of those he attracts from his sophisticated marketing are not the ideal patients for his philosophy, but he believes that if only 10% of those who inquire are accepting of his comprehensive treatment planning, it's money well spent.

Extensive advertising and promotion is necessary only for some dentists, namely those in the early stages of practice. As the patient base grows, dependence on marketing tactics should decrease. For the new practice owner, a budget of 2% to 5% of income is sufficient for ads and promotions. As the practice flourishes, this budget can be reduced to 1% to 3%. Once dentists have reached the point where they are fully booked for two to four weeks in advance, there is a temptation to reduce or eliminate ads and promotions. In fact, many dentists who completely eliminate their marketing budgets report little negative effect on their practices.

The established dentist, with 1,000 patients or more, needs little help to attract new patients. Referral will generate new patient flow of about 10 to 20 patients a month in most practices. Even after factoring in a patient attrition rate of 1% to 2% a year, a dentist's referral network will almost certainly result in an adequate patient base.

The authors' databases indicate some interesting figures about patient count and average income per patient per year. For example, many dentists are now generating over $1,000 per year per "active" patient. Spending on dental care in the U.S. in 2008 was $101.2 billion, this is projected to grow to $180.4 billion by 2019. The typical active patient is now spending about $500 per year on dental care. Therefore, the average dentist needs only 1,000 patients to earn about $500,000 per year in fees. There are many exceptions, such as young children, who have less need. Those dentists situated in low-income neighbourhoods, may require up to 1,500 active patients to earn a similar income, and dentists in high-income areas may be satisfied with as few as 750.

Income Hours

It is essential that dentists track their actual income hours and the resulting fees generated. Income hours refer to the hours spent at chair-side treating patients. Hours spent performing management duties are not included. The young dentist will work 1,500 to 2,000 chair-side hours, and should generate $150 to $250 per hour, given today's fee schedules. This will result in dental fees of $225,000 to $500,000 per year. As dentists become more experienced and their skills and efficiency improve, it's not uncommon to reach hourly production figures of $300 to $500 per hour, depending on the type of treatments performed. Some dentists, who have taken extensive clinical and continuing education courses, generate in excess of $1,000 per hour.

However, due to the long appointments required to generate higher hourly fees, they typically see fewer patients per day, thus allowing them to rely upon a lower active base. One of the drawbacks of their increasing hourly production is the propensity to reduce the ongoing needs of those patients. As the treatment plan reaches completion, patients' average annual spending will decrease as they enter the maintenance phase of their care. Dentists then become reliant upon their referral network. They may even resort to advertising and promotions once again, to renew adequate new patient flow and sustain their income expectation.

This process can become cyclical. Income increases, patient flow decreases; income declines and dentists seek to increase flow again. Many dentists suffer from this phenomenon, and it is a natural evolution through the mid-career stages of dental practice. As with any business, there will be years of surplus and years of decline, but the typical dentist will easily work through the cycle. When tracked over a ten-year period, it is evident that income hours and average earnings usually increase by 2% to 5%. Most fee guides allow for a modest increase in fees each year, to keep pace with inflation, and if the competency of the dentist is increasing, another 2% to 5% increase is not uncommon.

CHAPTER 22

Analysis of Dental
Practice Gross Income

For years, the U.S. Bureau of Labor Statistics and national dental organizations have commissioned studies to ascertain what the "typical" U.S. dentist earns. Most experts conclude that the average gross income, as of 2008, is about $710,000 per full-time solo general practitioner and $1,005,000 for a specialist.*

Research conducted by the authors from 1995 to 2005 supports this conclusion. This analysis, involving practices with a minimum of five years in operation, predicted average yearly gross income increases of 3% to 4%. Increasing patient demand, fee guide increases and other variables contribute to these averages. These findings, when projected further (assuming all factors remain more or less the same), suggest the typical U.S. dentist should be generating fees close to $850,000 in 2010 and doubling to nearly $1.7 million by 2020.

*SOURCE: 2009 ADA survey of dental practice income from the private practice of dentistry

These studies also confirm that the typical dentist retains between 35% and 45% of gross income on an adjusted cash flow basis. "Adjusted" means the various studies do not account for spousal wages (unearned) and non-reoccurring expenses such as major renovations, new equipment additions, extensive continuing education, legal fees and others.

As of 2008, the average net income for an independent private practice owner (solo or co-owner) was just over $207,000 for a general dentist and over $342,000 for a specialist.* By 2015, this should increase to just over $400,000. By 2020, average adjusted cash flow should be roughly $350,000 to $500,000. When compared to other professions, such as general medicine, accounting and law, dentists are presently earning 10% to 30% more, and this trend will likely continue. With this in mind, it is easy to see that dental practices will remain a popular choice for those seeking to obtain a professional degree!

CHAPTER 23

Suggested Fees and the Art of Scarcity

● ●

Dentists are provided with guidelines as to the fees they should charge in almost every state. This is a service provided by dental associations, consultants and insurance companies and it is a useful tool for determining fees that are fair for both dentists and patients. Fees are highly dependent upon the skill set and the ability of the dentist to communicate the worth of the service to the patient.

If the large majority of dentists charge similar fees regardless of experience, are the fees fair?

This is a sensitive topic particularly when discussed with older, experienced dentists. Many feel the practice of set similar fees is unfair as it does not recognize their experience and higher competency. In almost every other business, experience warrants higher fees. Those with greater skill and a wider scope of knowledge charge more than those with less. Lawyers, accountants and even dental specialists are evidence of this practice.

What Fees Are Fair?

The fee guide is ideal for the dentist with less than ten years' experience. Those who continually learn new techniques and expand their skills should be charging more than the suggested fees. How much more? Increments of 2% to 3% are not uncommon and several of our clients consistently charge 5% to 10% above the customary fees charged in their area. One client was charging 30% above the suggested fee for several procedures, including crowns. When informed that he may be the most expensive dentist in the community, he replied:

> *"I should hope so or there's something wrong with my service!"*

This potent reply concisely explains the belief that skills and ability are necessary to deliver optimum dental care. It might become the basis by which dentists explain their elevated fees.

Practicing the Art of Scarcity

As a dental practice grows, confidence and experience allow for increased demands on daily scheduling. Many dentists utilize auxiliaries to help with increased patient flow, such as expanded duty hygienists and level II dental assistants. When the ability to manage patient flow exceeds capacity, the temptation to hire an associate dentist then arises.

This is a wonderful opportunity to take the practice into one of two directions:

1. Group practice with two or more dentists
2. The refined solo practice

Group practice has much appeal to those who wish to continue to grow a patient base. The need for treatment can only be addressed by adequate dental manpower. Statistically, a large majority of dentists are unaware that they are actually losing money by employing associates. In his 2004 study of Ontario dentists, R.K. House, a well-known dental authority, reported that:

"In most instances, the Practice Owner is actually subsidizing their associate."

This is true because

- In the first year, practice owners lose money on newly trained associates as they have yet to perfect working within the practice, gain the trust of the patients and increase their competency to "get up to speed."
- In the second year, practice owners typically break even on associates when they effectively begin to share the patient load.
- In the third year, practice owners profit from associates.

Here's a fact that most practice owners neglect to consider:

The average tenure of an associate is less than two years!

The solo dentist with too many patients is very fortunate. The practice can be perfected and controlled, without the need for an associate dentist. Dentists can optimize their time while restricting their availability. This begins with the decision to remain as a solo dentist — the chosen model of over 75% of North American dentists. These dentists may reduce their need to increase patient numbers and rely on patients that suit their individual style. Many dentists interviewed relate five main reasons why they chose this model:

- Fewer patient visits per day
- Increased hourly income
- Lower staff turnover
- Higher professional satisfaction
- Less stress

Dentists are taught, from the beginning of their career, to attract new patients and to keep them. This is common for all businesses. However, in most businesses, capacity can be expanded to serve an increasing volume by adding machinery and staff. Dentistry is not compatible with this expansion theory. It is the dentist who must perform the bulk of the income-producing duties as only a limited volume of work can be delegated. When patients' needs exceed the dentist's availability, it's time to reduce the needs, not to increase the dental manpower. Scarcity is the art of being available, but not too accessible. Reducing hours, increasing fees and tightening the collection policies will lead to a reduction of patients to the point that the dentist's schedule is full, but only for the hours he/she wishes to work.

The term "compassion fatigue" was coined by a consultant who studied dental professionals. He found that the desire to be a health care provider often took priority over the desire to be a successful business person. Dentists should be commended for making themselves available for the care of their patients. However, at what point does this obligation become a burden? Dentists are known for giving too much of themselves, often at the expense of their own health. Dentistry has proven to be a high-stress occupation, and it should be remembered that all dentists must seek a balance between career and all other aspects of their lives, especially time with family and friends. When their appointment book is full and an emergency presents a high level of stress because of lack of time, then it is time to reschedule at a slower rate.

One client revealed that he had to work late most nights, rarely took a lunch and had little time for communicating with his patients. He was busy — very busy! He admitted that he did not feel that he was providing adequate care, as he could not enjoy longer appointments to treat his patients and meet their total needs. His year-end figures looked impressive, but there was a cost. He was gaining weight, sleeping poorly and showing many signs of burnout. His solution was to add an associate to relieve him of some of the excess work.

One year later, he had gained more weight and his wife indicated his health was suffering. He confessed that he had too many patients and not enough time to treat them. He believed that the goal of all dentists was to acquire a large patient load. To this end, he was successful, liked by his patients and he received many new referrals.

The young associate he hired was not intending to stay long term and was not particularly adept at handling a busy schedule. The dentist's stress level increased when staff and patients complained of long waits and backlogs. The situation became untenable when the associate moved on to a new opportunity.

The dentist had two choices at this juncture: repeat the process and hire another associate, or drastically cut back his work schedule. He felt selfish when he chose to reduce his hours. He was fearful he would lose the respect of his patients and suffer income loss.

One year later, the dentist had lost weight, appeared less stressed and was happy. What did he do? He raised his fees, reduced his hours and gladly referred those patients who were unhappy to another dentist. In effect, he set a target of fewer patients, not more! He reduced scheduling demands, saw fewer patients per day, and made longer appointments per patient — all resulting in higher fees.

The lesson to be learned is simple. Dentists must care for their own needs first before they can give quality care to others.

CHAPTER 24

Hiring an Associate

• •

The authors have always advocated strongly in favor of the solo practice. However, there are many dentists who at some point will hire an associate. When doing so, plan to do two things:

1. Enter into a written agreement.
2. Plan for the associate's departure.

While there are a few instances of successful, long-lived relationships between dentist and associate, the career associate is rare. Most dentists desire to be their own boss and wish to be so sooner rather than later. They are ambitious, energetic and can bring energy and new ideas to a practice. Rarely are the dentist and the associate in total agreement with regard to the philosophy of the practice.

From a positive perspective, associates can relieve the dentist of an excessive patient load, allow the dentist more time off and extend annual holidays. On the other hand, the associate needs help to learn the trade, gain experience and develop competency. This can only be accomplished if the dentist and associate work closely together. In many instances, this does not happen and the two dentists often find themselves on opposing career paths.

One young associate confessed that her employer was well educated, very competent and had much to offer. In the early stages, they shared caseloads and information and enjoyed an excellent working relationship. After a while, the associate began to feel neglected as the owner took more time away from the office — which was one of his reasons for hiring the associate in the first place. The associate became the predominant caregiver in the practice, assuming more responsibility than was first intended. She felt overworked and even mentioned that she was now responsible for management duties that were not officially delegated nor compensated for.

As she more or less became the lead dentist, the demands grew beyond her ability, given that she had only graduated a few years earlier. The staff began to feel neglected as she would postpone decisions until the practice owner could be consulted — something that became increasingly difficult to arrange.

The situation worsened when the associate discovered that she was pregnant and had an increasing need for additional time off for health reasons. She did not mention her situation to the practice owner for fear of being replaced. Then the practice really began to suffer. The staff could not manage all the patients with the decreasing dentist schedule. The dentists were not adequately supervising the office, as neither could devote adequate time to the business, and patients felt they were being unfairly put off for needed care.

The staff finally approached the practice owner after numerous patient complaints. What was he to do? He enjoyed a luxurious, part-time work schedule and a well-developed personal lifestyle. The office had generated a reasonable profit for over a year, and it afforded him a comfortable income.

With reservations, he decided that it was time to return to full-time practice to catch up on the backlog. In doing so, he reunited with many long-standing patients who began to express their concerns about the lack of attention and delayed appointments. Out of duty to the patients, his schedule then increased rapidly — much faster than he was mentally prepared for. Once again, he found himself in need of an associate, and he questioned the wisdom of repeating his earlier choice to hire one in the first place.

He decided that two part-time associates would be the solution, so as to reduce the risk of having a similar experience. Within six months, he had secured two such associates.

Ironically, the first associate he had hired delivered a healthy baby and asked if she could return to the practice about six months afterwards. Now the practice owner had three part-time associates, all of whom he felt obligated to keep busy. He then returned to his limited schedule, working only one or two days a week and once again taking several months off, all the time thinking he had regained the ideal schedule.

Then, about one year later, with all three part-time associates showing positive signs, he made the difficult decision to sell the practice and exit dentistry altogether. To his dismay, not one of the part-time associates was interested in buying the practice — they all had other career plans in various stages of development. Sadly, when the practice owner announced his intentions to sell, each associate accelerated his/her other plans, giving notice of leave one shortly after the other. As tensions grew and each dentist's objectives grew further apart, the practice once again suffered.

After a year-long process, the owner managed to identify a suitable candidate to purchase the office and take over all the management duties.

The post mortem of this transaction reveals that the office sold for less than it was worth, the owner was subjected to several years of rapid change in lifestyle and workload and all the dentists ended up feeling somewhat disappointed that their intentions, while honorable, were never respected by the others.

CHAPTER 25

Upgrading the Facility and Equipment, and the Issue of Overcapitalization

● ●

Every practice requires upgrades at some point in its lifespan. In some cases, it may be 10 or 20 years before major equipment needs replacing. Certain items last longer than others, such as dental chairs, stools, x-rays and cabinets, while some need replacing more frequently, such as hand pieces, curing lights, sterilizers, x-ray developers (for traditional film) and computers. When upgrading, resist the temptation to purchase a new technology unless it can prove that it will speed delivery of care, improve patient comfort or increase profitability. The suppliers have extensive training to help the dentist with these decisions.

Upgrading a Facility

What impression does your office leave with your patients? Dental office design and décor have changed dramatically over the past 20 years. Numerous observations reveal that some older offices have outdated and undesirable appearances, while other offices are opulent, fashionable and even extravagant. The key is to strike a balance between the image that is desirable and the investment required to make it so. When deciding, experience suggests a conservative décor so as to prevent patients from assuming that you are charging fees to pay for the extravagant surroundings.

The location, community and profile of your patients have bearing on décor. Whether you're serving a middle-income or a higher-income clientele, it is prudent to be modest! Do not subscribe to the overly flamboyant style of office décor unless it suits your individual personality and you are able to remodel as styles and fashion change.

One practice visited in 2005 had invested over $1.5 million in technology, décor and equipment. It was stunning. Highly regarded patients were asked what their impressions were. They commented that the facility was incredible and they were impressed with their new dentist's commitment. However, when pressed, they wondered if the fees they were paying were above the norm to pay for such facilities. An examination of the dentist's most recent financial statements revealed that the fees charged were actually in keeping with the fee guide for the area. However, the impression of a high-cost practice had already been formed in the patients' minds and they were skeptical. In summary, most dentists should decorate with style and with modesty. The exceptions to this rule are those dentists who have the desire to be seen as the most advanced in the profession.

Overcapitalization

One unfortunate side effect of over-investing in the practice is the theory of diminishing returns. Essentially, this economic principle dictates that dentists will only be able to earn a certain level of fees, regardless of the investment made. Patient flow, the nature of their patients and community demographics dictate that dentists will only be able to generate a certain level of income, no matter how much they have spent on the office.

Years of observation and research suggest that investment in the practice should not exceed an average figure of one year's gross income. An average of the last three years of gross income should be used to calculate this figure. If investment exceeds this amount, then the practice is overcapitalized. New dentists should use the projected average gross income for years five and beyond to determine how much to invest. Only about 29% of the dentists in the U.S., in relative dollars, grossed over $1 million in 2008.* The authors' findings suggest that many dentists have invested more than is required and are experiencing diminishing returns.

Selling the Opulent Practice

Overcapitalization carried to an extreme creates an opulent office. These ultramodern, high-tech offices are impressive to many of today's young dentists. When

*source: ADA survey on dental practice in 2008.

compared to the facilities they trained in at dental school, it is easy to see why.

Upon closer investigation, many young dentists become intimidated by high-tech offices and often say they could never afford to buy such an office. The finance companies also have some resistance to these operations. Even if the cash flow supports the investment, they have serious concerns about the novice dentist's ability to replicate the cash flow to afford the high costs of debt service and maintenance.

While these modern offices remain saleable, it is often at a diminished return to the owner. Due to the reservations of both buyers and their financiers, the offered price is often lower than the reasonable fair market value, if only due to the conservative nature of the cash flow projections they make when investigating a purchase.

Comparatively, the modest office, with total investment of less than one year's average gross, will almost always produce adequate cash flow, even for the young buyer, and financing is obtained in most instances.

While there are always exceptions, the ratio suggested here to determine overall practice investment is a result of long standing observation and analysis.

CHAPTER 26

Continuing Education: Perfecting Clinical and Communication Skills

· ·

There are more courses available to the dentist than ever before. One ROI client discovered that the number of lectures available in a year was over 250. Most of these were clinical, but some were of a business nature. The majority of clinical courses focused on aesthetics, implantology and endodontics. The most common business course focused on patient communication skills — for both dentists and their staff. Educators know that dentists lack training in these areas, and they offer a wide array of choices to fill this need.

Clinical continuing education helps dentists to improve their speed of delivery and to provide a wider scope of treatments. However, there are limits to what a dentist can do in any given day. One client had taken so many courses that he became confused as to what he could offer his patients. He had purchased a number of devices that expanded his scope of treatment, but could only find time to use one or two of them regularly. While he was a competent dentist, he was over-whelmed with the options he had learned to offer.

Over time, he became resolved to subspecialize in a few areas beyond traditional restorative treatments, and found himself referring out the usual amount of work. He accidentally became overeducated, to the point where he had difficulty choosing what his core competencies were. It's tempting to study and learn from the experts, however

A wise business owner knows exactly what they do best, and they attempt to perform it often. The wiser business owner knows when to refer work out!

If there is one course of non-clinical study in which the dentist should enroll, it is the art of communicating with patients. All dentists know how to speak in dental terms, but some have great difficulty effectively listening to patient concerns and addressing them.

The typical patient enters a dental office with pre-conceived notions of dental care, some that were formed many years before today's modern techniques were developed. Many patients have fears and anxieties about visiting a dentist.

Communication is paramount to gaining patients' trust and cooperation in maintaining good dental health. With this thought in mind, all dentists are advised to take courses designed to improve their skills in relating to their patients and minimizing patient fears and uncertainties. In doing so, dentists' case acceptance rate will increase, as will their profits.

LEAVING THE BUSINESS PROFITABLY

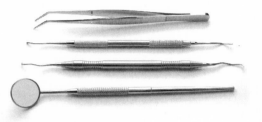

CHAPTER 27

The Art of the Appraisal

The appraisal document is the factual presentation for numerous financial and legal issues. The appraisal defines what the dentist has built for himself/herself and what it is worth in today's market. It is not a management report of suggestions for future growth.

A professional appraiser, with his/her accreditations, standards and no conflict of interest, will assure the client of quality work and complete confidentiality. His/her objectivity ensures that readers of the appraisal (accountants, lawyers, bankers, insurers and potential buyers) can do so with confidence.

The appraisal can be used for many purposes: insurance, estate planning, borrowing of funds or refinancing of existing funds, buying another practice (sometimes they merge together) or a family business transition. All of these purposes need the appraisal statement to document the value of the practice.

The authors' philosophy of the appraisal has always been that it is designed, written and formatted for the intended reader. The intended reader is a specific dentist. Lawyers, accountants, bankers, consultants and family members also read appraisals, but the intended reader is the dentist.

Thirty or forty years ago the appraisal was not necessary because dental practices were not worth anything. Why would you pay $1,000 in 1972 to have your practice appraised if it was only going to sell for $5,000?

As the market has developed, the need for appraisal has grown simply because the value of dental practices is getting higher and higher. At the time of publication, practices are selling for hundreds of thousands to millions of dollars. It is understandable that a bank, a lawyer, an accountant and a purchaser would want a proper appraisal.

Owners are sometimes reluctant to invest in the appraisal because they have a pretty good idea what their business is worth. Their accountant may have given them some advice, or they may have heard about other transactions of classmates; for example, "His business is just like mine so it is probably worth $500,000." A buyer will not accept that.

When people sell their house, the first thing they do is interview two or three real estate agents. A part of that process is not only interviewing them and their marketing plan, but also finding out what the house is worth. In effect, they are getting two or three appraisals before they list the house.

Why would professionals not invest in a proper appraisal so that they know where they stand? This is particularly important if a dentist is thinking of transitioning a practice.

Appraisals have become an absolutely essential planning tool. For the sale of the business, it is mandatory. But it is also becoming a mid-career planning tool. "If my business is worth half a million today, what will it be worth in ten years? Will I be able to retire at 57 or 66 or whatever my retirement plan might be?"

Appraisals are also becoming an elective product that dentists are pursuing in mid- or late-career to explore the question, "What are my options?"

The Process

In our experience, it takes about a month for a professional appraisal firm to prepare an appraisal from start to finish. It is necessary to identify, document and assign value to the various goodwill factors involved in the practice as well as accurately record the details of all major company assets: manufacturer, value, serial number, age, condition and color.

An appraisal usually remains valid for about one to two years. This depends on major market fluctuations, which are not that common in dentistry. It also depends on whether the business goes through rapid changes such as expanding, bringing on new staff, buying new equipment, taking over the suite next door or moving across the road to buy a whole new building.

Experience dictates that the appraisal should not be

free, even though some firms do offer it as part of their sale package. The fee normally charged is about $5,000 for the appraisal and a separate fee for the sale. Appraisal fees are 100% tax deductible. A reputable professional appraisal will save the dentist both time and money since it is far more likely to be accurate and serve as a usable document.

Essentially, the appraisal fee and the sale fee can be likened to how dentists run their businesses. Patients who go to a dentist to have their teeth cleaned do not expect a rebate if they come back a few weeks later for a couple of crowns. These are separate services, even though they are performed at the same office.

Current Users of Appraisals

Years of observation reveal that there are two groups of dentists. There is the 65+ club, which might be referred to as the traditional generation of dentists. Then there is the baby boomer generation. The boomers are the planners and consumers of professional services. They hire investment advisors, appraisers, brokers, accountants and consultants.

The senior generation is a more do-it-yourself generation. Their thinking has been forged by a post-depression belief in frugal self-reliance. They fix their own equipment. They mow their own lawn. They change the oil in their car.

These dentists will do their own appraisals, often at their peril. They are likely to be inaccurate and unacceptable to purchasers. They will try to sell their own practice using a FSBO (For Sale By Owner) venue. This same practice often occurs in real estate markets reflecting the same skepticism about the need for professional help and guidance.

As mentioned, the boomers are far more likely to hire a professional appraiser. They recognize that the appraisal has become a necessary means of doing business. They are prudent, and also recognize that they cannot leave their practice to their family in case of death.

66% of all small businesses in the U.S. have no exit strategy in the event of their disability, retirement or death.* With an appraisal, dentists or their estate can sell the practice.

Seven Uses of Professional Appraisal

Below are a number of uses of an appraisal for a dentist's practice:

1. Establish selling price for outright purchase or baseline for buy in/out.
2. The appraisal may be reviewed with an accountant or other practice advisors to identify any opportunities for improvement or change.
3. The appraiser can meet with dentists or their advisors to explain his/her methodology and to assist dentists in preparing a "critical path" plan.
4. The "minus" adjustments portion of an appraisal is found on the calculation of the goodwill page. These benchmark comparisons are the negative aspects of the practice as purchasers see it. Some of these items can be changed to increase the value of the

---

*SOURCE: 2009 Harris interactive study

practice at little or no cost.

5. A copy of the appraisal should be stored with a dentist's other valuable documents when steps 1, 2, 3 and 4 are complete. The dentist should attach a Letter of Instruction (see Appendix F), which can be prepared as part of the appraisal, that will help in the event of his/her sudden death or disability. A Last Will and Testament should also be included.

6. To increase the practice income, experienced appraisal companies can recommend companies and individuals that teach fundamental techniques to help dentists achieve this goal.

7. Years of service in the appraisal business generates a national list of accountants, lawyers, bankers, insurance professionals and practice management consultants who can help with the next phase of the dentist's career, whatever it may be.

CHAPTER 28

Selling the Business

Dentists sell their practice for one of three reasons:

1. *Sickness* — The dentist has developed a serious health problem. Many dentists will hang on in the hopes that they will get well and either work part-time or put in a temporary dentist to help them while their health improves. This is understandable but usually a mistake. Approximately 75% of dentists who go on major disability will not come back to work. If they hang on to their business in the interim, that business will suffer. Experience suggests selling the business and taking the necessary steps and time to get well. If full health is restored, the dentist is free to start again with the benefit of hindsight.

2. *Sick and tired* — "That's enough dentistry for me. I've done this for 30 years, I'm moving on."

Sometimes it is after 40 years or even just 20 years, but for some dentists there comes a time when they choose to move on. Many dentists who are tired of full practice go into academia, consulting or part-time dentistry as a non-owner. This can be seen as PTFL (Part-Time For Life) and FFO (Freedom From Ownership). Dentists who choose this route of PTFL and FFO can travel or work in different places. They can work a month and then take a month off as a temporary locum dentist. There are many ways to stay in dentistry without staying chained to a five-days-a-week full-time dental practice and all the responsibilities that come with it.

3. *Financial freedom* — Many dentists have achieved financial freedom because of successful saving and investment plans. Some inherit wealth or have financially successful spouses who make retirement possible. These dentists are the freedom 55 or younger group that can move on from a dental career to do other things.

In the U.S. as of 2007 35% of all professionally active dentists are over fifty-five years old.*

At this point, the projection is that there will *not* be enough buyers to meet the supply of dental practices for sale. The likely result is that prices for practices will fall. This may be evident by 2012.

Today in 2010 we have more buyers than sellers in hot urban markets and cities with dental schools. The market is quite high — the highest it has ever been. It is safe to say that prices for practices have increased

*SOURCE: Distribution of dentists in the United States. American Dental Association, 2009

dramatically in recent years and are likely to peak somewhere between the years 2012 and 2015. In rural areas prices are declining.

Thereafter, there will likely be a slow diminishing of value for dental practices because there are too many dentists selling at once and not enough dentists in line to meet the oversaturation of opportunities.

One possible mitigating factor is a large number of foreign-trained dentists moving to Canada to requalify. They join the third- and fourth-year students at various universities and graduate with the same degree as a traditional dental student.

These dentists are highly motivated, in mid-career and have families. They have mortgages and debts that make them willing to work long and hard hours. Foreign-trained dentists are excellent buyers of dental practices.

These new graduates and foreign-trained dentists should be convinced or encouraged to move to rural Canada. In doing so, their practices would certainly be very lucrative and personally rewarding.

For Sale By Owners

What does a dentist do to sell his/her practice? Assuming the appraisal is completed, the dentist may or may not then retain the services of a broker.

Although it is becoming less popular, For Sale By Owner (FSBO) still exists. The reason that people try to sell their own practice is to save the commission. However, there is huge risk to selling something on your own — you are unrepresented by a third party.

The main risk is the accidental withholding of

information. Both the purchaser and owner do this without even recognizing it. The purchaser is afraid to ask questions, because he/she does not want to insult the owner. The owner is not certain what to volunteer and many issues go unaddressed.

This accidental withholding of information can turn into negligence that can turn into purposeful misrepresentation, which may end in litigation. Generally speaking, it is all quite innocent yet very costly to the seller.

Both professionals do not want to insult each other. The younger one does not want to insult a senior. A senior does not want to insult a junior because he or she is a potential buyer. Thus, the For Sale By Owner has a very high failure rate.

Dentists, like most of us, are humble, and when they are selling something on their own, they do not want to be seen as too pompous or arrogant or overly confident in themselves or their services. They do not want to appear too aggressive to a buyer. The result is that dentists undersell themselves and their practices.

Dentists accidentally neglect to recognize the strengths of their business as the market sees it. Unknowingly, they can withhold some of the weaknesses of their business and not expose pertinent information unless asked.

Using a Broker

A broker can explain the weaknesses of a practice and highlight the strengths in ways that an owner cannot.

The broker can be more honest (not as modest as an owner) and use the appraisal document to its fullest to support the asking price.

The broker can suggest to late-career dentists how much to improve their practices' environment, equipment and overall appearance before sale. Many dentists often say, "I hear what you are saying. Those are great ideas. I'm tired and I'm ready to sell. Let the next guy do it. If I have to spend an extra $50,000 to sell my practice to earn an extra $100,000 a year later, I would rather sell it today. Let the buyer spend the $50,000 and let them do the work the way they choose. I do not want to live through the renovations."

Experience and many years of observation suggest that this course of action is, in fact, the best. If dentists enhance their practices before selling, they make changes based on what they think is best, rather than what the buyer thinks is best. For example, they may purchase a dental software program that the buyer has found wanting and inadequate. Comments like: "This is the worst dental software program I have ever seen. I am in a practice today that uses it and we do not like it," are common.

Therefore, sellers should not anticipate what buyers want since they do not know who the buyers are or their preferences. It is better to sell sooner, save the money and effort and let the new owner enhance his/her new practice in his/her own way.

In preparing a business for sale, dentists should remove all clutter and personal touches (such as family photos and personalized greeting cards). Old equipment is perfectly good if it is working. Some items may need only cleaning, paint touch-ups and other minor cosmetic changes. It is not necessary to spend a lot of money on improvements.

Those who advise a dentist to spend a lot of money just before they sell to increase the "value" of the practice may be doing so out of self-interest. They may have been serving this dentist for 20 or 30 years and want to end the relationship with a lucrative sale.

It really is best to let the buyer make the decisions about upgrades and long-term purchases.

If the owner decides to retain a broker, there are a number of firms to choose from. Commissions range from a low of 6% up to 10% and by and large reflect the age-old wisdom that "you get what you pay for."

The broker will then advertise the practice and search out potential buyers. Most brokers have a list of "buyers in waiting." In fact, all brokers have the same list because buyers check out each of the brokers. Unlike residential real estate, there are no exclusive "buy only through me" agreements in dental practice sales.

There are no multiple-listing services. Many buyers call all brokers. They have no need to be loyal to any broker. The one that provides them with the best practice in the best location for the right price within their time frame is the broker they will use.

The broker will then start interviewing potential purchasers, qualifying them, and ascertaining their interest and their financial capacity. They will look to see if there is a match between a certain practice and how it is run. They look at location, geography (urban versus rural) and where the buyer's family is located.

There are many reasons someone might be attracted to a certain practice, so brokers try to pre-qualify the buyer as best as possible. A broker will selectively and carefully take qualified buyers to see the office. All showings are done after hours. A dental practice is rarely shown during working hours.

The main reason for this is that the staff should *not* know the practice is for sale. Dentists should never tell staff the business is for sale until the identity of the purchaser is known and the sale is unconditionally final.

To tell staff that the business is for sale, without telling them who is taking it over, often leads to unnecessary fear and uncertainty. They will not know who is taking over and if their jobs are secure.

The time for staff to know that any business has been sold is when the transaction is unconditional; that is, there is no going back for either party. At this point staff should be notified and all obligations as determined by the state employment law must be met. Most buyers keep the existing staff because it helps to retain the patients of the purchased practice.

In some instances, when a buyer has seen the practice after hours — note that the buyer has *not* met the dentist selling the practice as yet — the buyer takes the appraisal to his/her accountant for assessment, then to a banker to see about financing, and then, if the buyer is serious, he/she starts talking to the broker or perhaps to a lawyer about drafting an Offer to Purchase.

From the moment the dentist decides to retain a broker to sell his/her business to the point where an

Offer to Purchase is drafted may take from one month to a year. It depends on the location of the practice, the style of practice (general dentistry versus more expensive cosmetic dentistry) and the overall size of the practice. A longer time frame may be required for specialty practices.

There are many factors that can impact the demand for the business. Today, in particular, demographics and geography are the main factors. Many buyers want to be in major urban centres. In major urban practices, the selling process is usually shorter than in rural or remote communities.

As a courtesy by the broker, a draft is often drawn up and then sent to the buyer and his/her circle of advisors for review, discussion and modification. An Offer to Purchase document usually results.

Once an offer has been drafted, the buyer signs it first and his/her deposit is affixed. The broker delivers it to the seller. The seller is usually given a week to make a decision (consulting with his/her advisors — an accountant and a lawyer). The seller has three options:

1. Accept the offer as is.
2. Reject it outright (which is very rare).
3. Make a counter-offer (which is the most common response).

The counter–offer is simply a message that says: "I accept the bulk of your terms but I would like to change the date or perhaps the price and negotiate some of the conditions." Once mutual agreement is reached, an Accepted Offer of Agreement to Purchase and Sale is prepared.

The agreement then goes through a 10- to 15-day conditional period where the purchaser is allowed to do final inspections of the office, verify that his/her financing is available, and contact the landlord to make sure the premises lease is satisfactory.

If the building is owned by the dentist (which is the case about 30% of the time), it is sold as part of the deal from one dentist to the other and usually requires a property appraisal and a building inspection.

The closing date is 30 to 90 days from the Accepted Offer of Agreement to Purchase and Sale.

Patients are not notified until the closing date and the seller has the buyer's money. Informing patients of the pending sale leads to confusion and uncertainty, especially if something goes awry. It is important to minimize any uncertainty for patients, staff, landlords and suppliers by using a well-thought-out process that a professional broker can provide.

Once the deal is unconditional, the staff are notified of the buyer's intentions. Other things to be done include notifying insurance agents and advisors, and preparing letters to patients about the change of ownership and the closing date.

Seller and Buyer Working Together

Experience suggests that in nine out of ten transactions, the owner should not stay on and associate with the buyer. Some brokers recommend the very opposite and encourage an "after sales" relationship between new and old owners.

Documentation reveals that the seller and buyer are usually from different generations and different cultures, have different training, went to different universities and have different philosophies and different needs.

If the previous owner stays on with the pretense that it will help with patient retention, the buyer now has a dentist working for him/her who cannot change his/her ways. The patients and staff will gravitate to the old dentist out of convenience and habit. Ironically, the buyer still has to pay him/her to be there.

Patients go to a dental practice for many reasons and, as previously mentioned, the dentist is *not* the main reason. This is a sobering fact and the seller must come to understand that anyone is replaceable.

Follow-Up After Sale

Reputable firms act exclusively for the seller. However, it should be remembered that every buyer is a potential client for the firm in 20 or 30 years. To ensure satisfaction, a reputable firm will survey purchasers one year after the sale to learn what has happened with the practice. Two questions should be asked:

1. Did your patient count go up or down?
2. Did your revenue go up or down?

Based on years of surveys, it can be concluded that buyers will retain 85% to 95% of the previous patients.

In addition, their own marketing and presence can substantially increase the number of patients overall.

On average, revenue after one year is up 10% to 15%. In some cases, the revenue increase is much higher, usually because of the younger dentist's desire to get out of debt and make the practice profitable as quickly as possible.

Buying a dental practice is a prudent, proven investment, and the vast majority of dentists survive and prosper in the first year. There are many survey examples revealing that dentists have doubled their billings and revenue in one year. There are few investments that rival the purchase of a dental practice by a highly motivated young dentist.

Revenue Growth

The U.S. population is aging and will require more and more dental services. Increasingly, the U.S. population understands the need for dentistry for cosmetic reasons.

The many advances made in cosmetic surgery procedures have caused a remarkable increase in cosmetic dentistry. The baby boomers want to look good and are willing to spend the money on whatever procedures they believe will enhance their overall appearance. This was not the case with previous generations and bodes well in both the long and short term for dental practices.

Five Things You Should Do When Buying a Dental Practice

1. Prospective sellers should call all of the brokers that advertise in *ADA Journal*. Sellers are obligated to contact each broker because brokers do not share their listings with each other like residential real estate agents do. In other words, there's no Multiple Listing Service (MLS) and if you only call one broker, you will not be aware of all the different opportunities available to you.

2. In order to investigate the entire market of practices for sale, dentists should also write or call each of the For Sale By Owner advertisements. These are private sales. They can usually be found in the classified advertisements and they sometimes use a box number at the magazine to screen their inquiries. Unfortunately, it takes a long time to get a reply from a box number, and sometimes you get no reply at all because private sellers receive dozens of letters from all over the world.

3. Find a good accountant. He/she will become the dentist's most trusted source. The accountant will look at all the different financial information the dentist receives while investigating practices. Most accountants charge an upfront fee and/or an annual fee to help you find the right practice. They will also prepare proposals for the bank and help the dentist with personal and business tax planning.

4. It is important to establish a relationship with a financial institution. Banks or specialty practice lender companies are willing to review the appraisals dentists

have acquired to pre-approve their loan. However, these institutions are often reluctant to go through the entire credit application process until the dentist has shown them an accepted Offer to Purchase.

5. After looking for one to two years, a buyer may identify the "right" practice. At this time it is prudent to see a lawyer and begin discussing your Offer to Purchase. Most brokers will draft an offer for you, at no charge, and will e-mail, fax or courier it to your lawyer. The broker should also process and make the changes your lawyer wants in order to have the final offer ready for signature in triplicate.

CHAPTER 29

Trends and Predictions

● ●

"Change doesn't occur in our lives until the pain of living outweighs the pain of change."
— OMER K. REED, D.D.S.

There are important marketplace trends of which every beginning, mid-career and end-of-career dentist should be aware. The authors' predictions are based on decades of research and experience.

Peaks and Valleys

Between 2012 and 2015 the value of dental practices will peak. Then there will be a slow decrease in value for dental practices nationwide.

In rural and remote communities, practices will experience a more rapid decline simply because dentist profiles for 2010 to 2020 indicate that dentists do not want to leave urban centres. This same trend is evident in medical practices today.

Family physicians do not want to go to small rural or remote towns (no matter what incentive plans are put in place). It is not attracting them because their desired lifestyle may be found in the bigger cities. For the most part, economic incentives are not working. Thus, rural and remote practices will experience a decline in value of about 5% to 10% per year between the years 2010 and 2020. This is a most unfortunate development and will have great impact on rural dentists and patients alike. In some states we are seeing more regionalized medicine, where patients travel to urban centers to make a day of doctor visits and shopping.

Deregulation of Ownership Structures

The most apparent trend with regard to regulated professions such as dentistry is toward deregulation. Deregulation is evident with regard to pharmacists, real estate brokers, business brokers, optometrists, legal professionals and many other professionals. All have seen or are going to see less regulation in both ownership structure and owner privileges.

Already, anyone can buy and run a dental practice as long as licensed dentists are involved in management (ownership share) and perform the dentistry. There are several companies that follow this model, such as ADPI and Heartland.

Should deregulation occur as predicted, the value of dental practices will temporarily surge and three to five years later, values will drop more rapidly. What this means is that lay people (i.e. non-dentists) can invest and buy dental practices in the same way they can buy a Tim Hortons or McDonald's franchise. Owners do not have to work there — they only have to invest in them and hire staff to run them.

There is an emerging trend in dentistry where investor dentists merge or create a chain of practices. Within a couple years, there will be non-dentist investors who are buying practices and hiring dentists to do the work. They may possibly consolidate practices, bulk up a practice, do multiple purchases or create chains.

As a flood of new buyers enter the dental practice market, the value of practices will fluctuate. There will be a flurry of purchases, acquisitions and mergers. Then the market will surge and decline, as opposed to the long-term ramp-up that occurred up to now, followed by a long-term diminishing of values in the marketplace. Corporate chain investment activity has the potential to bring a massive spike followed by a decline in dental practice sales.

This type of buyer will run out of practices to buy and so there will be fewer sellers in a short time period. There are only so many properties for sale at any time. Regardless of price, many dentists will not sell their businesses and as a result, there will be a quick absorption of the existing supply for sale. The buying frenzy will be over.

There will probably be some decline in values and then the cycle could repeat itself again starting in 2020 and beyond.

Revenue Explosion
In 2010, the dental industry will generate about $107.9 billion retail dollars.* That is $107.9 billion in dental

fees for services that the U.S. public have consumed — 50% of which is covered by insurance companies and 50% of which is covered privately.

Statistics Canada reported that dentistry did $9.94 billion in 2007. The 2008 figures will easily exceed $10 billion and will probably end closer to $11 billion. A reasonable prediction for 2020 is that dentistry revenues will exceed $20 billion. In the U.S., a reasonable prediction for dentistry revenue in 2019 would be $180.4 billion.★

To a large and ever-increasing extent the revenue increases will be a result of increased cosmetic procedures. The boomer generation will live longer and require more of the aforementioned procedures. This is good news for the revenue side of dentistry.

Female Dentists

Female dentists will be the greatest single demographic that will change the landscape of dental practices for the next two decades. A female dentist will follow a similar career path to a male, with some exceptions:

1. 18–25% of all female practitioners work part time.
2. They prefer to work no more than twenty minutes from home.
3. 85% practice in urban or suburban areas.
4. They gravitate toward part-time associate practices more than males.

Dentistry will continue to attract an ever-increasing number of women in the profession. By 2020, 30% of all dentists in practice will be female.

★SOURCE: cms.gov website and ADA survey center

Foreign-Trained Dentists

Many of the faculties of dentistry across North America charge substantially higher tuition fees to dentists who emigrate from other countries to requalify here. American and Canadian students may pay only 20% to 30% of what a foreign-trained student pays annually (although Americans and Canadians must go for four years rather than the two years required of foreign dentists). For the 2008–2009 school year there were 590 foreign-trained dentists in U.S. dental schools.★

It makes economic sense to open more positions for foreign-trained dentists to come to the U.S. and Canada to requalify. Dental faculties can expand class sizes to accommodate these changes or they can allocate more positions to foreign-trained dentists, thereby reducing the number of spots available to Canadian and U.S.–born-and-raised applicants.

If dental faculties expanded the number of graduates in the coming ten years (both domestic and foreign trained), there would be an increase in the number of buyers in the marketplace. More buyers increases the value of dental practices the boomer generation dentists will be selling, while also providing more and more North Americans with their own dentist.

Advice from the Authors

. . . .

1. An astounding number of business owners do not have a will or a transition plan. Begin a practice with the end in mind. It is widely acknowledged that more than 65% of business owners have not planned for transition or created a will. Not only does this lack foresight with regard to your benefactors, it is a *colossal* oversight on behalf of your business. Get a will and have a transition plan!

2. If you suffer a serious illness, take the necessary time and actions to rectify this development. If necessary, sell your practice. Experience has shown that it rarely pays to try to keep the business going in a haphazard way or to use an associate to get you through the rough times. Should your health be completely restored and you so desire, start again with the benefit of hindsight. You have only one life! Enjoy the fruits of your labor.

3. If a short-term illness or disability occurs, it is wise to participate in a mutual aid death and disability group or have a locum dentist in your employ who can temporarily take over and carry the practice. Locums are becoming an ever increasing and popular way to deal with short-term illness or patient overflow.

4. Be aware of compassion fatigue and practice the art of scarcity when determining the hours worked and stress endured. Seek a balance between work and play. Be aware of burnout and realize that you can provide quality care only when your own personal needs have been met.

5. When selling a practice, never reveal your plans to staff or patients until the sale has been completed unconditionally. (Bonafide contracts in place and financing all approved.)

6. The vast majority of graduating dentists will prefer to locate in major urban and suburban areas. To date, no amount of incentives, by government and otherwise, has been sufficient to change this trend. However, it disregards the fact that there are a number of lucrative, creative and personally rewarding practices available in many non-urban centres across the country. It is estimated that by the year 2015, rural dentists will average well over a million dollars a year. Their overheads are always substantially lower.

7. The most successful form of dental practice is the solo dental practice. At least 75% of all practices fall into this category.

8. Young dentists seeking a dental practice to purchase must be cautious and patient. Finding the right practice for you takes time. Usually, the right practice will present itself to you. The right practice is one in which the clinical procedures and overall operation mirrors the purchaser's dental philosophy.

9. Most graduating dentists are not ready to buy an existing practice or establish a new practice of their own for at least three to five years. These new graduates often find success as an associate dentist in that interval.

10. Dentists opening a new dental office in a competitive popular area are likely to experience two years of expenses exceeding income. It is prudent to have sufficient financing in place so that this anticipated initial negative cash flow can be met.

11. The referrals you receive from your patients of their friends, family and acquaintances are crucial. Ultimately, it is the most important factor in growing a new dental practice. It pays to treat your patients well!

12. Be careful about discounting your fees for dental services. Once this practice becomes common knowledge, it is difficult in the future to charge what your service is truly worth.

13. Solo dentists should look for an office of approximately 1200 square feet. This size is optimal from the perspective of need, comfort and economy.

14. The dental office should be ergonomic and elegant in its simplicity, both in terms of its design and function.

15. Dentists should sit in their operating chairs and reception room regularly in order to see and feel what their patients experience. Often this leads to improvements in both service and office presentation.

16. The most important aspect of buying an existing practice is the patient base. In essence, this is the "business" you are buying. Elementary research can reveal much about the patient base, including the overall number of patients, as well as their gender, age, ethnicity and insurance coverage. Know what you are buying.

17. The face of dentistry is changing as more and more women enter into dental practice. In addition, more and more foreign-trained dentists will be an integral part of the North American dental profession.

18. Dentists should work in their areas of expertise and specialty and know when to refer other work to other dentists.

19. Cosmetic dentistry, especially as demanded by the so-called "boomer generation," will become the most lucrative part of most dental practices. Basic cosmetic procedures should become the structure upon which a practice is built.

20. The total investment in a dental practice in most instances should *not* exceed the average of three years' gross income. Any further investment results in a diminishing return on investment.

21. It is evident that investment in dental practice ownership will extend to non-dentists because of deregulation. Corporate-style dental chains will continue to emerge and become a significant part of dental practice.

22. Refrain from office romances. Maintain a friendly but professional relationship with all employees.

23. Communicate with your staff. Praise them for work well done. Gently remind them when they are not meeting your expectations and move on. Compensation should be based on industry standards, seniority and, most importantly, on quality of work.

24. All dentists should have a well-defined office policy manual. It should clearly define expectations between dentist and staff as well as inter-staff expectations. From time to time this manual should be revised and staff informed of any changes.

25. When considering the sale of your dental practice, it is essential that you employ the services of a professional dental practice sales firm. When it comes to selling their practice by themselves, dentists often underestimate and undersell their practices. Sometimes, quite innocently, they withhold critical information about their practice in terms of both its strengths and weaknesses. Hire a professional!

26. Many dentists state that they should have retired earlier. Know that there can be a meaningful and rewarding life after dentistry.

Appendix A: Curricula Vitae of Timothy A. Brown and Sarah K. Lynch

Timothy A. Brown

www.timothybrown.ca

Career Summary:

President & CEO, ROI Corporation www.roicorp.com
Dental practice appraisal, brokerage, financing, locum placement and consulting.

- Over 25 years of full- and part-time experience with a family-owned business.
- Broker of Record and Appraiser responsible for the opinion of fair market value for all professional practices evaluated by the firm.
- Established Locum Lifestyle™ concept of part-time dentists working short-term assignments in dental practices.
- Created Ethiclease™ (www.ethiclease.com), an equipment financing company.
- Conceptualized and trademarked i-Dentist™ and i-ROI™ for the growing market of third-party buyers investing in dental practices.
- Over 250 speaking engagements including: Canadian Dental Association, Ontario Dental Association, and many dental society meetings, dental study clubs and Canadian universities.
- Over 100 articles published in Canadian dental journals.

Account Manager 1987–1990
Specialized in financing for dental practice purchases with Healthgroup Financial (now CIT) and First City Trust. Negotiated mortgages, promissory notes, equipment leases

and credit lines. Negotiated the sale of franchised dental practices (Tridont Dental Centers) to new dental graduates and established practitioners.

Education:

- 1997–2011 — Mandatory Continuing Education
- 1996 — Professional Real Estate Brokerage, OREA
- 1996 — Certificate program, OREA
- 1995 — I.C. & I., Law, Mortgage Finance, OREA
- 1990 — Professional Selling Skills III (Xerox)
- 1989 — Dale Carnegie Sales program
- 1987 — Marketing Diploma, Sir Sandford Fleming College
- 1985 — Principles of Appraisal, Sheridan College
- 1984 — Real Estate as a Professional Career, Sheridan College
- 1983 — Secondary School Diploma, Mississauga Ontario

Sarah K. Lynch

www.JimKasper.com

Career Summary:

Partner, Jim Kasper Associates LLC, 1995–present
The leading practice brokerage and appraisal firm in the Northeast, specializing in appraisals and sales of professional practices and associate recruitment.

Administrator, Military Sales C&S Wholesale Grocers, Inc., 1987–1994
The Nation's leading wholesale distributor and logistics management company.

Mortgage Banker, Vermont Mortgage Group, Greenfield Co-operative Bank. 1982–1986

Leadership and Active Positions:

- Executive Committee — Past President ADS Transitions
- Director — Agora Staffing Exchange, Inc.
- Director — Coalition of Military Distributors, 1987–1994

Memberships:

- Institute of Business Appraisers
- Practice Valuation Study Group
- American Logistics Association
- Connected Health

Education:

- 1981 — A.A. Liberal Arts, Greenfield Community College
- 1983–1985 — Business Ed., University of Massachusetts and Franklin Pierce College
- 2000–2009 — Certified Yoga Teacher, RYA

ASSOCIATE EMPLOYMENT AGREEMENT

Agreement made this _____ day of _____, 20____, by and between _____,
who maintains a practice dentistry located at _____
_____ hereinafter referred to as "Employer",
and _____ of _____
_____, a dentist duly licensed to practice dentistry
in the State of _____, hereinafter referred to as
the "Dentist".

WITNESSETH:

WHEREAS, the Dentist desires to practice dentistry as an employee of the Employer, and

WHERAS, the Employer desires to employ the Dentist,

NOW, THEREFORE, in consideration of mutual promises Herein contained, the parties hereto agree as follows:

I

1. Employment and Term

The Employer hereby agrees to employ the Dentist on a full-time basis for the purpose of rendering, on behalf of the Employer, Professional Dental Services to such members of the general public asare, or hereinafter shall be, accepted as patients by the Employer, and the Dentist hereby accepts such employment. Patient treatment shall be performed on the days of _____, during the hours of _____. Additionally, Dentist is expected to be available to share in the treatment of patients on weekends and those patients in need of emergency care/treatment.

The term of this agreement shall commence on the above mentioned date and shall terminate as hereinafter provided.

2. Compensation and Other Benefits

The Dentist shall receive for Professional Dental Services rendered to the Employer the following remuneration and benefits:

(a) **Annual Compensation.** The Dentist shall be paid compensation in such amounts and at such times as set forth in "Schedule A" hereof.
(b) **Other Benefits.** The Dentist shall be entitled to such benefits as set forth in "Schedule A" hereof.

3. Duties

The Dentist accepts employment with the Employer on the terms and conditions herein and agrees that during the period of employment, Dentist will devote his full time and attention to the rendition of Professional Dental Services on behalf of the Employer to the furtherance of the Employer's bests interests. The Employer shall have the power to determine not only what specific duties shall be performed by the Dentist, but also the power to determine, within reason, the means and the manner by which those duties shall be performed. The following criteria beyond clinical capacities are important. They include commitment of time, productivity and efficiency in handling patient matters, willingness and effectiveness in

2

promoting the practice and oneself, actively assist in securing new patients, acceptance of practice burdens and responsibilities, including attending all meetings, interest in the practice from an entrepreneurial standpoint, clearly demonstrated ability to work with the Employer's members with good rapport and understanding and be responsible for the direction of the dental assistant assigned to the Dentist.

4. Business Expenses

The Employer will pay all normal operating expenses of the practice including office rent, utilities and the cost of reasonable dental supplies. In addition, the Employer will furnish, at it's expense, the following:

    (a) Adequate dental equipment and instrumentation;
    (b) One operatory shall be available to Dentist at all times, and other operatories available by schedule;
    (c) A full time dental assistant and access to the hygiene schedule;
    (d) Full support from the business office staff;
    (e) Professional liability insurance.

5. Accounting for Income

The Employer shall have the exclusive authority to fix, and to determine the procedure for fixing, fees to be charged to patients. All fees, compensation, monies and other items of value received or realized as a result of the rendition of Professional Dental Services by the Dentist shall belong to, and be paid and delivered to the Employer.

6. Assignment of Patients

The Employer shall have the exclusive authority to determine who will be accepted as patients, and the exclusive authority to establish procedures for designating which professional employee of the Employer will serve each and every patient, as well as the professional policies and procedures to be followed by the Dentist serving the individual patients assigned to Dentist, providing, however, that the

3

company shall not impose such employment duties, policies or procedures of any kind which would require the Dentist to infringe upon the Ethics of the Dentist's profession or violate any ordinance or law. The Dentist agrees to follow and abide by Ethics of the Dental profession and all federal, state and municipal laws and ordinances relating thereto or regulating the practice of dentistry.

7. Contracts

The Dentist shall have no authority to enter into any contracts binding upon the Employer, or create any obligation on the part of the Employer, except such as shall be specifically authorized by the company.

8. Expenses

The Employer shall reimburse the Dentist for the cost of professional society membership dues and continuing dental education expenses up to a maximum of Dollars per year. The Employer will reimburse the Dentist for all such expenses upon presentation by the Dentist, from time to time, of an itemized account of such expenditures.

9. Vacations, Professional Leaves and Sick Leave

The Dentist shall be entitled to an unpaid vacation and professional education leave, the length shall be set forth in "Schedule A", said vacation and educational leave to be taken at such time or times as shall be approved by the Employee. Additionally, the Dentist shall be entitled to sick leave and short term disability leave, the length of which shall be as set forth in "Schedule A".

10. Termination

The Employer or the Dentist may terminate this Agreement, without cause, upon sixty (60) days' written notice. Additionally, the Employer may immediately terminate the Dentist's employment upon the occurrence of one or more of the following events:

4

(a) In the event that the Dentist shall fail or refuse to comply with the policies, standards and regulations of the Employer from time to time established; or

(b) In the event that the Dentist shall be guilty of fraud, dishonesty or other acts of misconduct in the rendering of Professional Dental Services on behalf of the Employer; or

(c) In the event the Dentist shall fail or refuse to faithfully or diligently perform the provisions of the Agreement or the usual and customary services of his employment.

(d) In the event of a bona fide determination by the Employer to sell or reduce to cash substantially all of the assets of the Employer, or to distribute the Employer's assets to its members in liquidation, or to discontinue the practice of dentistry by the Employer: or

(e) In the event the Dentist ceases or otherwise becomes disqualified to practice dentistry; or

(f) In the event of the Dentist's Total Disability, as hereinafter defined. For the purpose of this Agreement, the term "Total Disability" as that term is used herein, shall mean the Dentist's inability on account of sickness or accident to regularly engage in or adequately perform his professional and other assigned duties hereunder. The term "adequately perform Dentist's duties", as that term is used above, shall mean the Dentist's inability to render Professional Dental Services for fifty percent (50%) or more of the Dentist's time which Dentist normally devoted to the rendition of Professional Dental Services prior to any disability. It is understood that the Dentist's occasional sickness or other incapacity of short duration may not result in the Dentist being or becoming "Totally Disabled" however, any illness or incapacity may lead to the Dentist being or becoming totally Disabled if he illness or incapacity is prolonged or recurring.

5

(g) Upon termination of employment hereunder the Employer will continue to collect, record and compensate Dentist for his work performed under the Agreement for a period of 120 days after the contract's termination. Any payment receive after the 120 day period will be retained in full by the Employer.

11. Relationship Between the Parties

The parties recognize that the Company shall manage the business and affairs of the Employer. The relationship between the Employer and the Dentist is that of Employer and Employee.

12. Access to Business Records: Disposition of Records, Files and Personal Property Upon Termination

Dentist's employment does not entitle Dentist to general access to the business records of the Employer. Dentist shall have access to the business records only to the extent necessary to verify compensation due Dentist from the Employer under the formula set forth in "Schedule A" of the Agreement, should a dispute arise with regard thereto.

If, for any reason the Dentist is no longer employed by the Employer, the records and papers of individual patients shall remain the property of the Employer unless a patient requests a different disposition thereof. Nothing herein shall prevent the Dentist from obtaining copies of records, at Dentist's sole cost and expense, of any patient of whom the Dentist was primarily in charge, and who may thereafter be treated by the Dentist.

The estate of the deceased Dentist shall not be entitled to any records or papers of an individual patient, nor any records of the Employer, except records or files relating to the personal matters of deceased Dentist.

13. Limitation of Practice

(a) In consideration of the benefits which will inure to

6

the Dentist by virtue of his employment by the Employer, the Dentist hereunder, however said termination may occur, and for a continuous period of _____ years thereafter, he shall not, jointly or individually, directly or indirectly, own, manage, operate, join in, control, engage or participate in the ownership, management, operation or control of, or be connected in any manner with, or directly or indirectly enter intothe employment of, any corporation, partnership, proprietorship or other type of organization or entity which engages in the practice of dentistry, nor shall the Dentist provide dental services, within a _____ mile radius of _____. The Dentist further agrees that he shall not, at any time, release, copy or otherwise make available to any person, firm, corporation, partnership, proprietorship or other business organization or entity any list of, or information relating to patients at any time treated either by the Employer or the Dentist.

In the event of a breach or threatened breach of any such covenants, the Employer shall have the right to enjoin the Dentist and his personal representatives, employees, successors, agents or assigns, from any threatened or actual activities in violation thereof. Dentist consents and agrees that temporary and permanent injunctive relief may be granted in any proceedings which might be brought to enforce any such covenants without the necessity of proof of actual damages.

(b) In the event that any of the covenants contained in paragraph 13 shall be held to be so broad in scope, area or duration as to be unreasonable and therefore unenforceable, then the provisions thereof shall be deemed to be reduced to such scope, area or duration, as the case may be, as shall be deemed to be reasonable and enforceable.

7

Additionally, the Dentist shall not, directly or indirectly, for his own benefit or the benefit of others, (a) divulge or disclose for any purpose whatsoever any proprietary information of the Employer including without limitation, lists or information regarding patients, employees, vendors, referring providers, procedures and charges of the Employer; (b) solicit any existing patient of the Employer; or (c) hire any existing employee of Employer.

14. Binding Agreement

This agreement shall be binding upon and inure to the benefit of the Employer and Dentist, and to their respective heirs, legal representatives, executors, administrators, successors and assigns.

15. Entire Agreement

This agreement is a contract and contains the entire understanding of the parties. Any interpretation of this contract will be made in accordance with the laws of the State of. It may not be changed orally but only in writing and signed by the party or parties against whom enforcement of any waiver, change, modification, extension or discharge is sought.

Date: _____   _____
                        Employer:

Date: _____   _____
                        Dentist:

8

SCHEDULE A

Dentist:

Time period of this Agreement

    Beginning:

    Ending:

Amount of compensation:

Compensation is payable on:

Duration of time away

    Vacation:

    Sick Leave:

    Continuing Education Leave:

    Short Term Disability:

Date: _____   _____

                                  Employer:

Date: _____   _____

                                  Dentist:

9

PRACTICE TRANSITION MANUAL

CONGRATULATIONS

On the Sale of Your Practice

It has been our pleasure to work with you to this end.

ROI CORPORATION IS 100% PRIVATELY OWNED AND HAS OPERATED IN CANADA SINCE 1974.

1155 Indian Road, Mississauga, Ontario L5H 1R8 Tel: (905) 278-4145 Fax:(905) 278-4705
www.roicorp.com

ROI Corporation Vendor Transition Manual ©

VENDOR'S ACTIVITIES FOR CLOSING

(After all conditions have been met)

1) **Assignment of Premise Lease**
   - ✓ Request Assignment of your Lease, or written consent to the assignment, from your landlord. (Your lawyer usually arranges this.)

2) **Meeting with New Owner**
   - ✓ Discuss Letter of Introduction & staff policies, scheduling etc.

3) **Staff Notices**
   - ✓ Advise your staff and deliver termination notices. Prepare "Records of Employment" as of closing. **DO NOT deliver notices until the Purchaser has removed ALL conditions.**

4) **Meeting with the Staff**
   - ✓ Schedule a meeting with the staff to introduce the new owner.

5) **Letter of Introduction**
   - ✓ Printing (photocopying).
   - ✓ Typing envelopes, labels or mail merge.

6) **Accountant**
   - ✓ Advise your accountant of the allocations of the purchase price.

7) **Telephone**
   - ✓ Advise Bell Telephone of change of ownership. They will send forms for signature.

8) **Insurance**
   - ✓ Advise Insurance Company of cancellation of appropriate policies (effective after closing date). Purchaser <u>may</u> assume existing policy.

9) **Rental Agreements**
   - ✓ Advise companies of cancellation or transfer (if applicable) of any rental agreements. Purchaser <u>may</u> assume leases.

Note: Once the Vendor and Purchaser have agreed on the wording in the introductory letter to the patients (which the Purchaser is responsible to mail as per the agreement), this letter, or any contact with the Vendor's patients by the Purchaser, should not be made until the sale has closed. This is to avoid any possible confusion or damage to the Vendor's practice in the very unlikely event that the sale does not close on time. The Vendor may agree to address and post a few envelopes in advance for those patients with appointments immediately following the close of sale.

PURCHASER'S ACTIVITIES FOR CLOSING

(After all conditions have been met and approximately one month before closing)

1. **Meeting with Vendor**
   - ✓ Draft the Letter of Introduction with Vendors input.
   - ✓ Discuss staff policies, scheduling, mailing (envelopes, stamps, labelling, etc.)

2. **Schedule a meeting with staff (Vendor is to set the date)**
   - ✓ Discuss offers of employment (terms, etc.) after all the conditions are removed on the Offer.
   - ✓ Take a photo of both dentists together in the practice.

3. **Rentals (assume/transfer)**
   - ✓ Rent (security deposit), etc.
   - ✓ Nitrous tanks, etc.
   - ✓ Computer software update.
   - ✓ Debit / Credit card machines (call your bank).

4. **Telephone**
   - ✓ Provide Bell Canada with your information after Vendor has notified them of transfer.

5. **Insurance**
   - ✓ Life, disability & fire, etc. effective date of closing.

6. **X-ray Inspection (HARP)**
   - ✓ Advise them of change of ownership.

7. **P. S. T. (not applicable in Alberta)**
   - ✓ Payable on equipment & furniture.

8. **G.S.T. (5%)**
   - ✓ Payable on leaseholds.

9. **Letter of Introduction**
   - ✓ Postage & mailing of letters on closing.

10. **Reception**
    - ✓ Plan a social function for departing dentist – invite patients.

11. **Stationery**
    - ✓ Personalized letterhead, envelopes, appointment cards, business cards, patient receipts, thank-you notes.

12. **Lawyer's Fees**
    - ✓ Searches, closing documents, registration.

13. **Accountant**
    - ✓ Submit P.S.T. & G.S.T. by 15th of following month of close (or as Accountant advises).

14. **Employer Number**
    - ✓ Go to: www.gc.ca/tax/business and register for payroll deductions.

15. **Advise suppliers**
    - ✓ Only **after** sale closes and keys in your possession.

ROI Corporation Vendor Transition Manual ©

PRACTICE PURCHASE

NEW OWNER'S STRATEGY

It is important to be aware of the patient's position on the sale of the practice. When a patient is coming to see a new dentist, it is usually because they have selected a dentist of their choice. In a practice transfer situation, the patient was offered no choice. Accordingly, they will be more observant and possibly more critical than if they had handpicked you.

Understanding this profile leads to two common sense rules for the new owner for at least the first visit:

1. Keep things the way they are as much as possible at first. The fewer the changes, the less the patient will have to absorb during their initial meeting with you. The more they can concentrate on you, the sooner they will satisfy their anxiety.

2. A step further than your Code of Ethics is to allow the patients to continue to believe that their previous dentist was competent. Remember, that it was their choice to have that dentist. Any indications that you are a "better" dentist may create a negative thought that the previous dentist was "not so good". This may be perceived to be a challenge to their judgement. For example: A sudden need for extensive dentistry may imply neglect on the part of the previous dentist. It may be more prudent to say that it appears the previous dentist was keeping this under observation but it now appears it is time to consider active treatment to head off any complications.

Any change in treatment and office procedures is more easily accepted if it is a result of some outside force, i.e. new fee guide, recent technology. Changes should be gradual and preferably after second or third visits.

Patient retention, on average, is about 85% – 95% after a sale. You can improve that percentage by taking the above two points into consideration.

These strategies have been compiled after reviewing the comments of hundreds of new owners we have worked with since 1974. This historical perspective is provided to you to minimize patient loss and maximize patient retention.

Here's To Good Dental Health To You And Your Patients!

P.S. <u>Renovations</u>:   It might be an idea to advise patients by newsletter of major changes and gently note that these changes will not result in any change of procedures/staff, but are a long term investment in their dental care and comfort.

Standard Wording

Stationery of Dr. _____ (Vendor)

Dear Patients -or- To My Patients:

I have had the pleasure of attending to your dental care for the past many years. Therefore, it is with mixed feelings that I have decided to:

- ❑ relocate closer to my home
- ❑ pursue other interests
- ❑ retire from dentistry
- ❑ retire for the betterment of my health
- ❑ slow down my dental career
- ❑ I want to personally thank you for your trust and confidence in me for the care of your dental needs.
- ❑ I want to personally thank you for permitting me the privilege of caring for your dental needs.
- ❑ I would like to extend my sincere appreciation to all of you.

I am pleased to announce that Dr. _____ D.D.S., will continue your dental care and will provide you with the same professional excellence that I have strived for.

Dr. _____ is a 19/20____ graduate of the University of, Faculty of Dentistry. Since graduation he/she has

_____

I am confident that you will find him/her to be a congenial and capable person.

- ❑ professional and personable
- ❑ is a highly regarded dentist
- ❑ having practised in _____ for _____ years.

We are
- ☐   personally acquainted
- ☐   have enjoyed a rewarding relationship both as a friend and colleague for some time.

All of your dental records will stay with the practice and the office telephone number will remain the same or will change to _____.

Ms. _____ will be continuing in the office to assist Dr. _____. She will be happy to receive your calls as usual and will ensure that your regular examination and recall appointments are maintained.

I know that I am leaving my patients and my practice in good hands and extend my very best wishes for your health and happiness.

Yours sincerely,

_____, D.D.S.

ROI Corporation Vendor Transition Manual ©

PRACTICE TRANSITION

When the Previous Owner is NOT With Practice or Unavailable

Suggestions of what to say to patients

Answer Telephone:

Initially, as **"Dental Office"** because the patient will expect to hear the **PREVIOUS** name, not the **NEW** owner's which may confuse them.

Explanation:

Dr._____ has retired, returned to school, or_____(other) and Dr._____ is the new Dentist.

The letter from Dr._____ announcing his retirement or _____(other) and introducing Dr. _____ to you, may not have reached you.

I believe you will find Dr. _____ both capable and considerate of your Dental Health.

All of your dental records, charts and x-rays are here. I would be pleased to arrange an appointment for you.

Dr. _____'s assistant (name) or/and receptionist (name) also our hygienist (name) has remained with the practice.

Suggested script to announce the sale of a dental practice to <u>Staff</u>:

We suggest that you schedule a staff meeting at the end of a short or light day of practice, and ideally when all staff can be present.

I have been very fortunate to have each of you to support this practice. I know that many of our patients comment about our team approach and how much they enjoy receiving their dental care from all of us.

Therefore, it is with mixed emotions that I have decided to A) Sell my practice and retire – or – B) Reduce my working hours and take more time for myself and my family (i.e. hobbies/travel?).

As you may already know, I have been searching for the ideal candidate to take over the patient load, and I want you to know that I was not certain who this individual would be until very recently. You may have heard some rumors, and I admit that some of them may have been true, <u>to some extent</u>, although I could not notify you until I was sure the 'right' dentist had been secured.

I have asked my chosen successor, Dr. _____ to introduce him/herself to you A) in a few moments – or – B) tonight/tomorrow. *(We recommended that the purchaser be introduced **within 24 hours** of this meeting).*

I have gotten to know him/her over the past few months and know that you will find him/her to be a wonderful, warm & caring dentist who will need your support moving forwards.

I will (will not) continue to work at the practice (If yes, mention the reduced schedule) and I will be available to help all of you, and the patients with this transition. I should also mention that I hired a professional firm who specializes in exactly this process, and the President, Timothy A. Brown has suggested I give you a copy of a column he wrote specifically about his company's experiences in these planned transitions.

If purchaser is to be introduced at this time: "I'm sure that you have questions, and I want to personally address each of them. But before we do that, I would like to introduce Dr. _____ to you – I think you'll really enjoy working with him/her!

This is a suggested script only – circumstances vary – contact your ROI Associate for more advice on this very important step in the process.

ROI Corporation Vendor Transition Manual ©

EMPLOYMENT STANDARDS INFORMATION

For more information on the Employment Standards Act in your Province please contact your local branch office.

You can also receive information off the Internet at the following websites:

Alberta Human Resources and Employment: www.gov.ab.ca/LAB/regs.html

B.C. Labour Employment Standards: www.labour.gov.bc.ca/esb/branch.htm

Manitoba Employment Standards Division: www.gov.mb.ca./labour/standards

Nova Scotia Labour Standards: www/gov.ns.ca/just/regulations/regs/lsc15496.htm

Ontario Ministry of Labour: www.gov.on.ca/LAB

Quebec Employment Act: www.dbic.com/guide/tm8-2.html

Mariana Bracic – Employment Lawyer – (905) 825-2268: www.mbclegal.ca

ROI Corporation Vendor Transition Manual ©

Canada Revenue Agency / Agence du revenu du Canada

Canada

Français	Contact us	Help	Search	Canada Site
Home	What's new	E-services	Site map A to Z index	Forms and publications

Forms and publications >

Forms and publications
GST/HST Policy Statements
P-166 Sale of Medical or Dental Practice Between Two Non-Registrants
Other formats

Please note that the following Policy Statement, although correct at the time of issue, may not have been updated to reflect any subsequent legislative changes.

GST POLICY STATEMENT

P-166 SALE OF MEDICAL OR DENTAL PRACTICE BETWEEN TWO NON-REGISTRANTS

Date of Issue

January 15, 1995

Subject

The GST treatment of a sale of a medical or dental practice between two non-registrants.

Legislative Reference(s)

Section 167.1, subsections 167(1) and 167(1.1) and paragraph 141.1(1)(b) of the *Excise Tax Act.*

National Coding System File Number(s)

11735-15

Effective Date

October 1, 1992

Text

Issue and Decisions:

Is the use of the election under subsections 167(1) and 167(1.1) of the *Act* necessary in the context of a sale of a medical or dental practice?

Where a person intends to sell a business, the vendor and the purchaser may qualify to file a joint election under subsections 167(1) and (1.1) of the *Act* to have no tax payable (with some exceptions) on the supply. However, the use of the above election may not be necessary notwithstanding that the conditions in subsection 167(1) are met but where both, the vendor and the purchaser, are non-registrants engaged exclusively in non-commercial activities. This may be the case with a medical or dental practice.

The sale of a medical or dental practice which constitutes a business generally involves the transfer of the following assets:

http://www.cra-arc.gc.ca/E/pub/gl/p-166/p-166-e.html

2/27/2007

(a) Medical and Dental Supplies and Equipment/Furniture

In general, sales of medical and dental supplies are either taxable or zero-rated. Sales of equipment and furniture are generally subject to tax.

However, the sale of personal property (which includes property that is not real property) is not taxable under paragraph 141.1(1)(b) of the *Act* if the property was acquired by the vendor exclusively (generally, 90% or more for non-financial institutions) for use in non-commercial activities and was not used in commercial activities.

It should also be noted that a doctor or dentist may qualify as a *de minimis* financial institution under paragraph 149(1)(b) of the *Act*. In this situation, the word exclusively in paragraph 141.1(1)(b) means 100%.

(b) Goodwill

Section 167.1 of the *Act* would generally apply to the supply of a medical or dental practice where, under the agreement, the purchaser acquires all or substantially all (generally, 90% or more) of the property required to carry on the business. Section 167.1 provides that the part of the consideration for the supply that is reasonably attributable to goodwill will not be subject to GST.

(c) Leasehold Improvements

Where a non-registered vendor, such as a dentist (or doctor) engaged exclusively in exempt activities, makes a taxable supply of real property/leasehold improvements to a non-registered recipient, such as another dentist (or doctor), the vendor must collect and remit GST on that particular supply. This would also be the case if a section 167 election was filed.

However, the vendor may be eligible for a rebate under section 257 of the *Act* for the GST paid on the vendor's acquisition of, and improvements to, the real property.

SAMPLE RULING - SALE OF ALL THE ASSETS OF A DENTAL PRACTICE

Statement of facts

A, who is a non-registrant dentist, has agreed to sell all the assets of his dental practice to dentist **B** who is also not registered for GST purposes. The closing of the sale will take place on March 15, 1995. The assets sold by **A** are as follows:

- dental supplies including various articles like crowns and caps;

- equipment and furniture;

- goodwill; and

- leasehold improvements

ROI Corporation Vendor Transition Manual ©

A previously acquired the above assets for use exclusively in the provision of exempt dental services, and in fact did not make any taxable supplies.

Ruling Requested

A is not required to collect and account for GST on the sale of the above business assets.

Ruling Given

Provided that the preceding statement constitutes a complete and accurate disclosure of all the facts, proposed transaction, and provided that the proposed transaction is completed as described above, our ruling is as follows:

The sale of dental supplies as well as equipment and furniture will not be subject to GST pursuant to paragraph 141.1(1)(b) of the *Excise Tax Act*. Furthermore, under section 167.1 of the *Excise Tax Act*, the consideration allocated to goodwill will not be included in calculating GST payable. However, A must collect and remit GST on the sale of the leasehold improvements since it is a taxable supply of real property. On the other hand, A will be eligible for a rebate under section 257 of the *Excise Tax Act* for the GST paid on the acquisition of, and improvements to the real property.

This ruling is given subject to the limitations and qualifications set out in GST Memoranda Series (1.4) issued by Revenue Canada and is binding provided that this proposed transaction (i.e., sale closing on March 15, 1995) is completed prior to June 15, 1995.

This ruling is based on the *Excise Tax Act* in its present form and do not take into account any proposed amendments to the Act which, if enacted, could have an effect on the ruling provided herein.

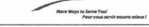

More Ways to Serve You!
Pour vous servir encore mieux !

Date modified:
2002-08-01

▲
Top of page

Important notices

ROI Corporation Vendor Transition Manual ©

Appendix D: Locum Agreement

THIS AGREEMENT made in duplicate this _____ day of _____, 20___

BETWEEN: Dr. _____ of the City of _____, the "**OWNER**"

- AND -

Dr. _____ of the City of _____, the "**LOCUM**"

BOTH PARTIES - THE OWNER AND LOCUM AGREE:

1. That this Agreement is made in good faith and strict confidentiality and with mutual trust and confidence.

2. That each party affirms that he/she subscribes to the Code of Ethics of the Canadian Dental Association and the rules and regulations prescribed by the Provincial regulatory body as the guide to his/her professional conduct in all relations with the other party, with other dentists and with patients.

3. That either party may terminate this agreement on giving twenty (20) days written notice.

4. That all fees charged, and accounts for professional services, shall be rendered in the name of the Owner. All amounts received shall be payable to and be the property of the Owner. Any cheques made payable to the Associate will be endorsed to the Owner.

THE OWNER AGREES:

5. To remunerate and pay the Locum _____ % of the fees charged and collected by the office for dental services the Locum performs after laboratory costs have been deducted. **OR**, to remunerate the LOCUM a daily rate of $_____ for each day worked, not to exceed ____ hours operatory time per day. **OR,** to pay an hourly rate of $_____ for each hour worked. Days and hours worked to be mutually agreed upon.

6. To remit payment to the Locum, in full, less agreed upon deductions, within ten (10) days of statement.

THE LOCUM AGREES:

7. To charge fees as suggested by the Owner and to abide by the policies of the practice.

8. That patients' records, charts, x-rays and models, including names, addresses and telephone numbers, will not be removed at any time, in any manner or way, without the Owner's written permission.

9. That he/she will not solicit any employees or patients of this practice to see work or treatment elsewhere.

10. That he/she will support the continuation of the practice during the sale, or the absence of the owner.

IN WITNESS WHEREOF the parties hereto have hereunder set their respective hands and seals.

SIGNED, SEALED AND DELIVERED, in the presence of:

}
}
}
_____ } _____ Date _____
Witness   Owner

}
}
}
_____ } _____ Date _____
Witness   Locum

_____

_____

_____

OFFER TO PURCHASE

Please be advised that the undersigned, _____

_____, _____, a dentist licensed to practice in

_____, Offers to purchase the dental practice of

Dr. _____ located at _____

_____. This offer to purchase includes all dental

equipment and supplies, furniture, patient lists and records, fixtures and other assets used

in connection with the said practice.

I offer to purchase the above assets for a total purchase price of _____

_____. This offer is contingent upon

and subject to the following conditions:

1)   The undersigned will deposit the sum of _____

to bind this offer pending the execution of a Purchase and Sale Agreement as

provided below. The deposit will be held in escrow by the Broker, Jim Kasper

Associates, LLC, P.O. Box 369, 11 King Court, Keene, New Hampshire 03431.

The undersigned will also provide_____in cash at time

of closing.

1

Other financing terms: _____

_____

_____

_____

_____

_____

_____

2) The Purchase and Sale Agreement between the undersigned and Dr. _____

_____And/or his legal representatives shall be entered into

within _____ days of the acceptance of this offer, and shall cover all

reasonable legal details of the transaction contemplated by this offer.

3) A complete list of all the assets of the practice will be attached to the Purchase

And Sale Agreement.

4) Agreement by the Seller, Dr. _____, to provide a

restrictive covenant not to compete or engage in the practice of dentistry on his

own behalf, as a partner, or as an employee, within a _____(_____) mile

radius of _____ for a period of _____

(_____) years beginning on the date of closing.

2

5) The Title to the assets must be free and clear of all materials liens and encumbrances, and the party accepting this offer must have full authority to Transfer the assets of the practice to the undersigned.

6) The Seller will provide a letter of introduction and endorsement to all active patients of record seen within the past year, for the benefit of the undersigned as his/her successor at the date of Closing, said letter to be subject to Buyer's approval as to form and content.

7) Accounts Receivable: _____

_____

_____

_____

_____

_____

8) Other Conditions: _____

_____

_____

_____

_____

3

This offer does not intend to cover all the legal documentation or other requirements which will be necessitated by this transaction. It is contemplated that a Purchase and Sale Agreement will be executed between the parties, covering all matters Not provided for herein. This offer is not assignable and will remain open until _____ _____. If the offer is not accepted by that time, the same will be withdrawn and the payment paid hereunder will immediately be returned. If you intend to accept this offer, please return a signed copy of this letter to me.

Thank you for your consideration of this offer.

Sincerely,

_____

The undersigned hereby accepts the Offer to Purchase contained in this letter, on This, the _____day of _____, 20_____.

_____
Signature:

LETTER OF INSTRUCTION – WHAT TO INCLUDE

1. Label on outside "Open Upon Death or Major Disability"
2. Copy to: Spouse/Attorney/Staff
3. Have Receptionist/Office Manager notify all other staff members
4. Office Manager/Receptionist should make contact with Spouse and/or surviving children for handling office
5. Review Death/Disability Manual if one exists
6. Contact Death/Disability Group if in one
7. Contact Practice Broker
8. Cancel patients for one (1) week telling them of the death or disability
9. Arrange for emergencies to be seen by Death/Disability Group or another Dentist
10. Complete and/or update Seller's Information Summary and gather the attached list of documents to be forwarded by the listing broker
11. Notify the following people:
    a. Attorney
    b. Accountant
    c. Letters to patients – when to send and what to say
    d. Letters to referring doctor, if applicable
    e. Malpractice carrier
    f. Closest professional colleagues
    g. Others:

12. What to do with practice income – checking/savings/money
13. Need supplies to continue operations
14. Bills to be paid (will depend on office)
15. Arrange for delivery of lab cases
16. What work is to be started?
17. What should be done about new patients
18. Complete existing treatment plans
19. Complete an inventory of equipment and supplies
20. Where to locate assets, passwords etc.

Appendix G: Buy Versus Set-Up Comparison

OPTION #1
Setting Up a Brand New Practice from Scratch
• This comparison will assume the dentist who sets up a new office will work full time in his/her new office.
• If he/she chooses to associate elsewhere, revenues in the first year may be lower.
• Rent is typically higher for new locations (storefront facilities) than for established practices renting in more traditional locations.
• Marketing expenses are generally much higher for a new practice.
• Wages in a new practice will be approximately
> — $15 to $20 per hour for a full-time receptionist
> — $14 to $17 per hour for a part-time assistant
> — $32 to $37 per hour for a part-time hygienist
• Miscellaneous costs in a new practice are low due to the new owner's tendency to conserve cash and avoid excessive spending.

Disadvantages
• Lenders have strict financing conditions since new practices are a high risk with no proven cash flow.
• Long hours with no profit for one to two years.
• Many non-billable hours in a new practice spent waiting for new patients.
• Working evenings and weekends.
• Dental supply costs in a brand new practice are very high in the first year due to the purchase of long-lasting items that are not considered consumables (single use).

OPTION #2
Buying an Established Practice
• Lenders grant long-term loans with fewer conditions on a practice with proven cash flow.
• Less staff training is required.
• More billable hours per week due to many pre-booked patients.
• Nine-to-five hours.
• Hygiene is independent and needs little attention.

Disadvantages
• Less ability to mold staff into your "ideal" office.
• Wages are often higher due to long-term staff.
• Practice might need an equipment upgrade or renovation to modernize, resulting in office down time, temporary closure to complete renovation and new equipment installation.

	Option 1		Option 2	
GROSS INCOME	**Set up NEW**		**BUY a Practice**	
Per Month	20,000		50,000	
Per Week (48/year)	5,000		12,500	
Per Day (225/year)	1,067		2,667	
Total Hours per Year (1,575)	152		381	
GROSS INCOME BY PRODUCER		%		%
Owner	200,000	83.3%	420,000	70.0%
Hygiene	40,000	16.7%	180,000	30.0%
TOTAL GROSS INCOME	**240,000**	**100%**	**600,000**	**100%**
EXPENSES				
Fixed				
Rent, Utilities & Business Taxes	48,000	20.0%	36,000	6.0%
Insurance - Office & Liability	4,250	1.8%	4,250	0.7%
Telephone, Marketing & Promotion	12,000	5.0%	6,000	1.0%
Dues & Licenses	2,350	1.0%	2,350	0.4%
Debt Service (see below)	76,320	31.8%	91,152	15.2%
Subtotal	142,920	59.6%	139,752	23.3%
Variable				
Staff Wages	72,000	30.0%	155,400	25.9%
Dental Supplies	21,600	9.0%	36,000	6.0%
Laboratory Fees	7,200	3.0%	42,000	7.0%
All Other (office, repairs, etc.)	19,200	8.0%	30,000	5.0%
Subtotal	120,000	50.0%	263,400	43.9%
TOTAL EXPENSES	**262,920**	**109.6%**	**403,152**	**67.2%**
NET CASH FLOW	**(22,920)**	**-9.6%**	**196,848**	**32.8%**

CALCULATION OF DEBT SERVICE

	Set-Up NEW	BUY a practice
Investment Amount	$450,000	$600,000
Term (7 years or less for new set-up loans)	7	8
Interest Rate (Prime + 1%)	5.00%	5.00%
Monthly Payment	$ 6,360	$ 7,596
Total Annual Payments	**$ 76,320**	**$ 91,152**

Christen, A.G., & Pronych, P.M. (1995). *Painless Parker: A dental renegade's fight to make advertising ethical.* Canada: American Academy of History of Dentistry.

Clapp, G.W. (1916). *Profitable practice.* New York: The Dentists' Supply Co.

Cloutier, E. (1947). *Dental supplies: Investigation into an allied combine in the manufacture & sale of dental supplies in Canada.* Canada: King's Printer & Controller of Stationery.

Dickerson, W.G. (1992). *The exceptional dental practice.* Reprinted 1996. Las Vegas: Las Vegas Institute.

Domer, L., & Berning, R. (1992). *Valuing a practice: A guide for dentists.* U.S.A.: American Dental Association.

Downie, J., McEwen, K., & MacInnis, W. (2004). *Dental law in Canada: A complete introduction to Canadian dental law.* Canada: Lexis Nexis Canada Inc.

Ehrlich, A. B., & Ehrlich, S.F. (1969). *Dental practice management: The teamwork approach.* U.S./Canada: W.B. Saunders Co.

House, R.K. (1970). *Dentistry in Ontario: A study for the committee on the healing arts.* Toronto: The Queen's Printer.

Howard, W.W. (1975). *Dental practice planning.* St Louis: The C.V. Mosby Company.

Jacobi, H.P. (1967). *A dentist's flight manual to success.* Revised 1974. Wisconsin: Project P. Inc.

Kilpatric, H.C. (1974). *Work simplification in dental practice: Applied time and motion studies.* Philadelphia: W.B. Saunders Co.

Layman, G.A., & Redmond, P. (1977). *As your practice grows: How to hire an associate, form a partnership, build a group.* Tulsa: Petroleum Publishing Co.

Philips, E.S. (2008). *Your Guide to the Perfect Smile.* Toronto: ECW Press.

Robbins, D.M. (2008). *Tales from the trenches: What you ought to know about selling your business — 14 alternatives to selling out.* Canada: Robbinex Inc. http://www.robbinex.com.

Schulman, M.L. (2000). *Change your practice successfully.* Rome, New York: Canterbury Press.

green press
INITIATIVE

ECW Press is committed to preserving ancient forests and natural resources. We elected to print this title on 30% post-consumer recycled paper, processed chlorine-free. As a result, we have saved:

12 Trees (40' tall and 6-8" diameter)
4 Million BTUs of Total Energy
1,117 Pounds of Greenhouse Gases
5,377 Gallons of Wastewater
326 Pounds of Solid Waste

ECW Press made this paper choice because our printer, Thomson-Shore, Inc., is a member of Green Press Initiative, a nonprofit program dedicated to supporting authors, publishers, and suppliers in their efforts to reduce their use of fiber obtained from endangered forests.

For more information, visit www.greenpressinitiative.org

Environmental impact estimates were made using the Environmental Defense Paper Calculator. For more information visit: www.edf.org/papercalculator